FamilyCircle®

Successful Microwave Recipes

The Family Circle® Promise of Success

Welcome to the world of Confident Cooking, created for you in the Australian **Family Circle® Test Kitchen,** where recipes are double-tested by our team of home economists to achieve a high standard of success—and delicious results every time.

MURDOCH BOOKS®
Sydney • London • Vancouver • New York

C O N T E

Eggplant Parmigiana, page 88

Vegetable Purées, page 29

Lemon and Olive Chicken, page 65

Ratatouille, page 30

N T S

The test kitchen where our recipes are double-tested by our team of home economists to achieve a high standard of success and delicious results every time.

Chocolate Puddings with Crème Anglaise, page 101

Warm Seafood Salad, page 12

The Publisher thanks the following for their assistance in the photography for this book: House in Newtown; Home & Garden on the Mall; Le Forge; Corso de Fiori; The Pacific East India Company.

Front cover: Pasta with Spring Vegetables, page 89; Cauliflower au Gratin, page 31; Beef in Red Wine, page 73
Inside front cover: Italian Mushrooms; Bean, Asparagus and Prosciutto Salad, page 40

When we test our recipes, we rate them for ease of preparation. The following cookery ratings are on the recipes in this book, making them easy to use and understand.

A single Cooking with Confidence symbol indicates a recipe that is simple and generally quick to make—perfect for beginners.

Two symbols indicate the need for just a little more care and a little more time.

Three symbols indicate special dishes that need more investment in time, care and patience—but the results are worth it.

Fish in Parchment, page 53

Spaghetti with Meatballs, page 70

Introducing the Microwave

Microwave ovens have been in our kitchens for many years now, but for most of us they are still simply a means to defrost chicken in an emergency or warm up a forgotten cup of coffee. The microwave oven should be far more than that—it is a quick and fuss-free way to cook real family meals.

Apart from the obvious advantages of speed, the shorter cooking times with the microwave oven also mean more flavour and nutrients left in the food. Because it cooks faster, the microwave oven uses less energy and produces smaller electricity bills. It doesn't heat up the kitchen and, for most of us the biggest advantage, there is never very much washing up—food doesn't stick to the dishes and a lot of the time you'll find you're preparing, mixing, cooking and serving, all from the same pot. Hopefully, this collection of family meals cooked in the microwave will prove to all of us that it can be used for everyday cooking. There are some dishes which obviously aren't at their best when cooked in the microwave—roasts are not a good idea and bread is to be avoided—but the recipes we have chosen have all been double-tested in our kitchens to ensure that they are as good as, or even better than, those cooked in an ordinary oven. There are no second bests included here, and anyone who's ever laboured over the stove and whisk to make a less-than-successful Hollandaise sauce will be thrilled with the unbelievably simple microwave recipe.

WATTAGE

All our recipes were devised and tested on an 850 watt microwave oven. At present, microwave wattages range from 500 on older models to 950 and are changing continuously. Check the wattage on your oven—it will be given on the front or inside edge of the door or at the back of the oven. The higher the wattage, the faster the food will cook so, if necessary, adjust the cooking times a little. If your microwave is more powerful you will need to reduce the times by a minute or two. If it is a less powerful model, add a minute or two.

The golden rule to remember with microwaving is that undercooking can be easily rectified, overcooking can't.

There are different power settings on a microwave oven, just as on a conventional oven—High (100%), Medium High (70%), Medium (50%), Medium Low (40%) and Low (30%). Just as on a stove top you wouldn't boil a stew at high temperature for a long time, neither would you do so in the microwave. Always follow the recipe instructions for correct cooking.

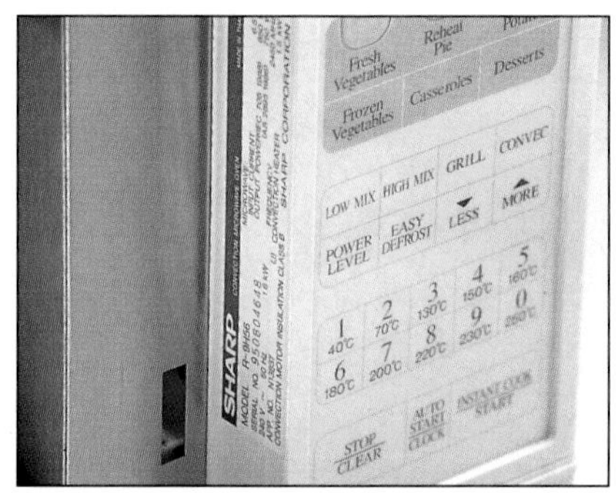

The wattage can sometimes be found on the back or inside edge of the door.

HOW THE MICROWAVE OVEN WORKS

The heart of a microwave oven consists of a tube called a magnetron. This converts ordinary household electricity into microwaves which are then directed into the oven cavity. The microwaves pass through the surface of the food and vibrate the molecules inside to create instant heat. The microwaves can only penetrate a few centimetres into the food so, as in conventional cooking, the centre of the food is cooked by conduction of heat. Microwaves are attracted to fat, sugar and moisture, in that order, so food containing a lot of fat will cook very quickly, while watery food may cook more slowly. People used to be scared that they were going to be 'microwaved' when taking food out of the oven, but when the oven door is opened the magnetron instantly ceases to generate microwaves and they do not remain in the food.

Do not turn on your oven when it is empty, or you will damage the magnetron. If you have small children who may turn it on by accident, always leave a jug of water in the oven, just in case.

ARCING

Arcing occurs when metal blocks the passage of the microwaves and causes sparks to appear in the oven. This also happens if metal or aluminium foil touches the top, bottom or sides of the oven while it is operating. Repeated arcing can damage the oven.

MICROWAVE-SAFE DISHES

There's no need to rush out and buy special cooking dishes for your microwave. The kitchen cupboard is probably full of bowls and casserole dishes which are ideal. All ovenproof glass containers are suitable. Do not put anything metal into the microwave—this includes dishes with gold or silver trims and enamelled pots which have metal cores—but most other materials will be suitable. Even paper or plastic plates, wooden or

You will find that most of the dishes in your cupboard are suitable for use.

wicker baskets can be used for just warming up food. You can test if a dish is suitable for cooking in the microwave by placing a jug of water in the microwave and putting the empty dish beside it (but not touching). Heat on High (100%) for 1 minute. If the water in the jug is hot and the empty dish cold then it is suitable for microwave cooking. If the empty dish is hot it has a high moisture content and is not suitable for microwaving. If it is warm, use the dish for reheating only.

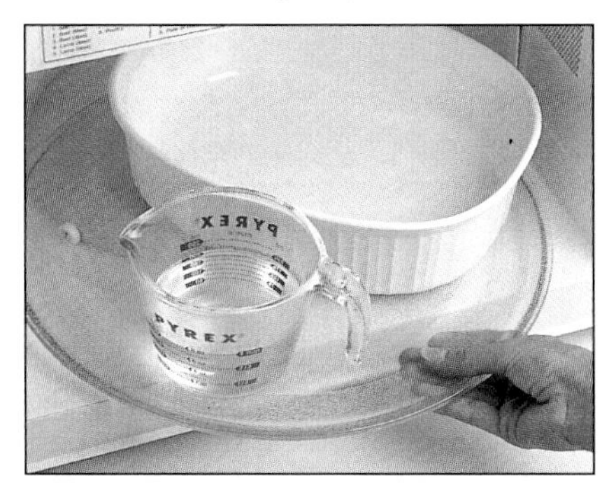

Test a dish by putting in the microwave next to a jug of water.

Round containers are best for microwaving as they receive an even amount of microwave energy. Square containers tend to accumulate heat in the corners and overcook there.

You will notice in some recipes that you are instructed to use a dish which is both microwave-safe and ovenproof or heatproof—this is because the food may be browned under a grill after microwaving, to give a crisp finish.

A word of warning: even though the dish itself should not heat up in the microwave oven, it will do so through contact with the food it contains. Always use oven gloves when removing dishes from the microwave.

PIERCING

Any foods with a skin or membrane need to be pierced before being cooked whole in the microwave. The classic example of this is the baked potato, whose skin must be pricked before cooking to avoid pressure building up and causing it to burst (in exactly the same way that we pierce sausage skins before grilling to prevent them bursting open). Unshelled eggs should never be heated in the microwave.

ARRANGING THE FOOD

On a hot-plate the centre of the pan is the hottest, but in a microwave oven the food around the outside of the dish cooks the quickest. Always cut food into even-sized pieces and place it in a circle so that it cooks at the same rate. Put the thickest, so slowest cooking, part of the food towards the outside of the dish—so chicken drumsticks, broccoli florets or whole fish would all be arranged with their thinnest parts pointing towards the centre of the dish. When cooking two ingredients of different sizes, for example cauliflower florets and peas, arrange the larger food around the edge of the dish and the smaller in the centre.

Cut food into even pieces and arrange in a circle, thinnest bits to the centre.

Arrange the food in circles, with the smallest at the centre, for even cooking.

STIRRING

Simple as it may seem, stirring is one of the most important techniques in microwave cooking. Because food around the outside of the dish cooks fastest, it needs to be stirred or rearranged to ensure even cooking. With stews and casseroles, always follow the instructions for stirring as it also helps the dish to thicken.

COVERING

The golden rule is that any dish which you would normally cover in the conventional oven or on the stove top should be covered (either with a lid or with microwave-safe plastic wrap) in the microwave. Some people are tempted to cover everything they put in the microwave, but this just means that they are steaming rather than cooking, so follow the instructions in the recipe. Just as on the stove top, some dishes should be cooked uncovered to allow liquid to reduce and thicken.

You will find in a few recipes you are required to cover a dish tightly. This means with a close-fitting lid or a layer of microwave-safe plastic wrap. If instructed to 'cover' or 'cover loosely' you should use plastic wrap and leave one corner unsealed or make a couple of holes in the top with a sharp knife. When a dish does produce a lot of steam, make sure you remove the wrap away from you to avoid steam burns to your face.

Contrary to popular belief, aluminium foil can be used to cover small areas of food in the microwave

Cover a dish with plastic wrap, leaving one corner loose for steam to escape.

A lot of steam may build up, so lift off the plastic wrap away from your face.

oven. The foil must cover less than 30% of the food (it is useful for very thin bits such as chicken wings or the tail of a fish, which may otherwise overcook) and must never touch the side of the microwave oven.

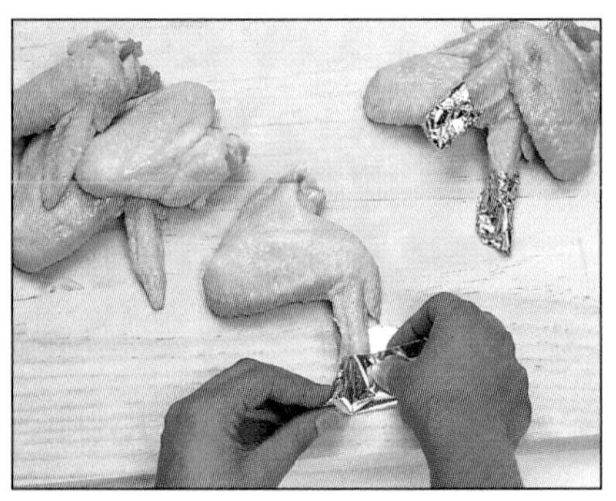

Very small amounts of foil prevent thin pieces of food from overcooking.

Sometimes food is covered with paper towel while cooking. This is often food which may spit or release a lot of fat as it cooks. Check that your paper towel is microwave-safe: some recycled varieties are not.

AFTER COOKING

In many recipes you will be instructed to leave the dish to stand for several minutes before serving. This is an important part of microwave cooking—the heat that remains within the food causes it to continue cooking. Always follow these instructions in the recipe, as the standing time has been taken into account when calculating cooking times.

BROWNING

One of the problems associated with cooking in the microwave is that the food doesn't brown and get a lovely crunchy finish. There are several ways to get round this. Sometimes meat or vegetables are basted or coated with seasoning before cooking to give a brown finish. Microwave browning pans are also available but it is just as simple to use a frying pan. Combine the speed and efficiency of microwave cooking with the crunchy smoky results from the frying pan or grill by browning meat or vegetables in oil in a pan first or flashing a cheesy or breadcrumb topping under a hot grill after cooking.

COOKING MEAT IN THE MICROWAVE

Many people who have had a microwave oven for years are adept at cooking vegetables and soups but steer clear of cooking meat. Cooked in the wrong way, meat dishes can be tough, dry and lacking in flavour. But cooked in the right way, stews and casseroles can be particularly succulent and flavoursome—we are very proud to have included a chapter of meat recipes which really work.

As stated earlier, fat cooks faster than anything else in the microwave. You will usually be instructed to first cut off any excess fat from the meat to ensure even cooking.

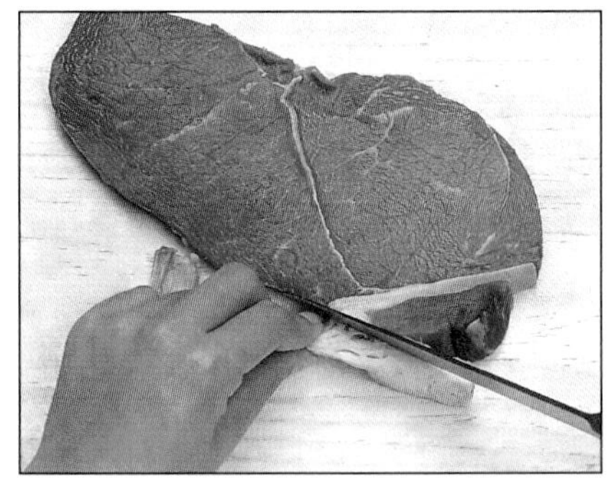

Cut away any fat from the meat before microwaving, so the dish cooks evenly.

In most cases the meat is cut into even-sized pieces and browned in oil in a frying pan before being added to the other ingredients and cooked in the microwave. This is to seal the meat and give it a good appearance and taste. When browning meat, if you have a small pan or a large amount of meat, always fry it in batches. If the pan is overcrowded the meat ends up stewing in its own juices rather than frying to a brown finish.

Brown meat in a frying pan in batches to give a good colour and flavour.

In most recipes you will find the meat is then added to other ingredients and liquid in a bowl and microwaved for some minutes, stirring regularly. This is the equivalent of simmering a stew or casserole on the stove top or in the conventional oven and it is at this time that the flavours blend and mature and the meat softens and takes on the flavour of any spices and herbs which have been added.

Because of the shorter cooking time for microwave recipes there is less time for the flavours to develop, so you will find we have usually advised to leave the dish to stand for at least 10 minutes after cooking to allow this to happen. As with all stews and casseroles, whether cooked in the microwave or conventional oven, you will get the best flavour if you cook them the day before, allow to cool, then refrigerate and gently reheat.

CLEANING

Forget all the other advantages of the microwave over the conventional oven—all you really need to know is that it is a joy to clean. Simply put a large microwave-safe bowl or jug full of water into the oven, add a touch of lemon juice and a drop of ordinary washing-up liquid and boil on High (100%) for 20 minutes. Do not cover or the water will boil over—also you want to produce lots of moisture. Remove the jug and wipe over the oven with a damp cloth—the dirt and grease will all have been loosened. Never use a commercial oven cleaner to clean the microwave oven.

ADAPTING RECIPES

One thing to beware of with microwave recipes is that you can't just double the quantities to make double the amount, as with conventional cooking. Liquid slows cooking times and, as stated earlier, fats and sugars cook at different rates, so the equation is not straightforward. Also, it is useful to remember that, although in a conventional oven two fish would take the same time to cook as one, in the microwave they will take proportionately longer—they are both now sharing the same amount of microwaves, so each receiving less.

Microwave Magic

The microwave is a fabulous time-saving tool in the kitchen at the best of times, but there are some fiddly occasions when it really seems to perform magic.

MAKING CHILLI POWDER

Cut chillies in half and de-seed. Chop roughly and place on a paper towel, on a microwave-safe plate. Cook in 2 minute bursts on Low (30%), until dry. Grind to a powder in a food processor, or mortar and pestle, taking care not to inhale the fumes.

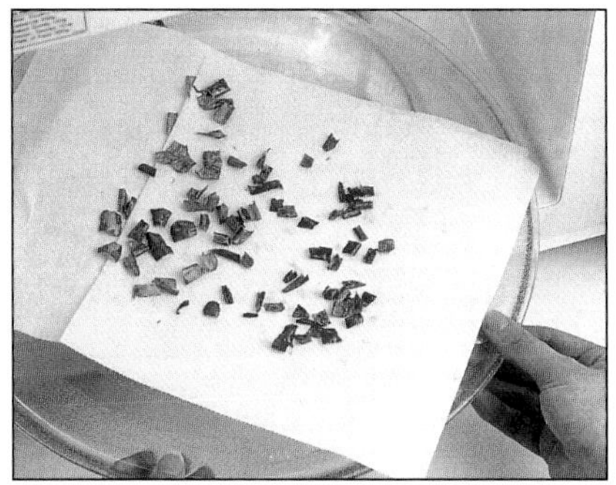

Roughly chop the chillies and place on a paper towel on a microwave-safe plate.

QUICK PORRIDGE

Combine 1 cup (100 g/3⅓ oz) instant rolled oats with 1 tablespoon sugar in a large microwave-safe bowl. Add 2 cups (500 ml/16 fl oz) boiling water, and stir to combine. Cook for 1 minute 30 seconds on High (100%); stir, then cook for a further 30 seconds. Stir again and leave for 3–4 minutes before serving. Serves 2.

Stirring the porridge will ensure that it cooks evenly.

GLAZE FOR FRUIT TARTS

Instead of making a time-consuming glaze, simply spoon some apple baby jelly into a small microwave-safe bowl and heat for 1 minute on High (100%), or until liquid. The jelly will set on cooling but can be reheated. Spread over the tart with a pastry brush.

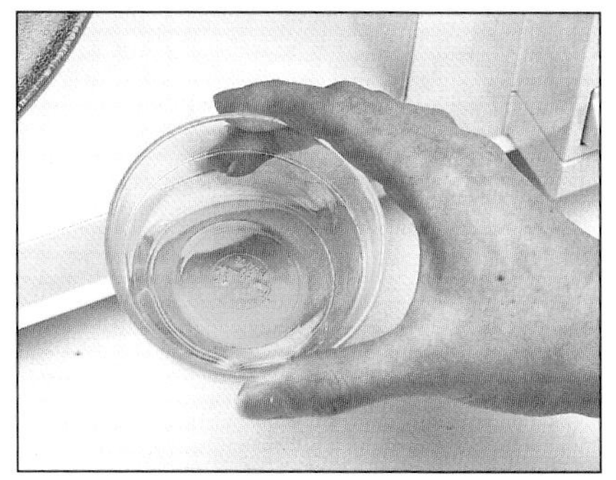

Baby jelly dissolves into liquid when heated—ideal for glazing fruit tarts.

DRY BREADCRUMBS

Remove the crusts from day-old slices of bread. Process the bread into crumbs, then place on a microwave-safe plate and cook in 1 minute bursts on High (100%), stirring often, until the crumbs are dry but not coloured.

Cook the breadcrumbs in 1 minute bursts, stirring often, until dry.

For toasted breadcrumbs: Melt about 20 g (⅔ oz) butter for each ½ cup (40 g/1⅓ oz) fresh breadcrumbs in a glass pie plate. Add the breadcrumbs and stir to coat with butter. Cook in 1 minute bursts on High (100%), stirring frequently, until the breadcrumbs are lightly golden.

MELTING CHOCOLATE

Melted chocolate is useful for decorations such as chocolate curls or coated leaves. Break or chop chocolate into small pieces and place in a microwave-safe bowl. Cook in 30 second bursts on Medium (50%), checking frequently. Chocolate holds its shape when melted in the microwave, so it may retain its squares—check by stirring. Don't stir the chocolate vigorously, and don't be tempted to try to cook it faster on a high heat, as it burns easily.

Chocolate melts in the shape of the pieces so stir to check, rather than overcooking.

SOFTENING HONEY

Warmed honey is more liquid, and easier to measure out when needed for recipes. Remove the lid from the honey jar and heat on High (100%) for 30 seconds, or until runny. Use as required. If the honey starts to set again, simply reheat. The rest of the jar can just be returned to the store-cupboard to be used again.

Heat the honey in the jar until it is runny and easy to work with.

TOASTING COCONUT

To toast coconut, flaked almonds or sesame seeds, spread them out on a microwave-safe plate. Cook in 1 minute bursts on High (100%), stirring often, until lightly golden.

Cook in 1 minute bursts, stirring often, until lightly golden.

PEELING GARLIC

Heat cloves of garlic on High (100%) for 40 seconds to peel more easily.

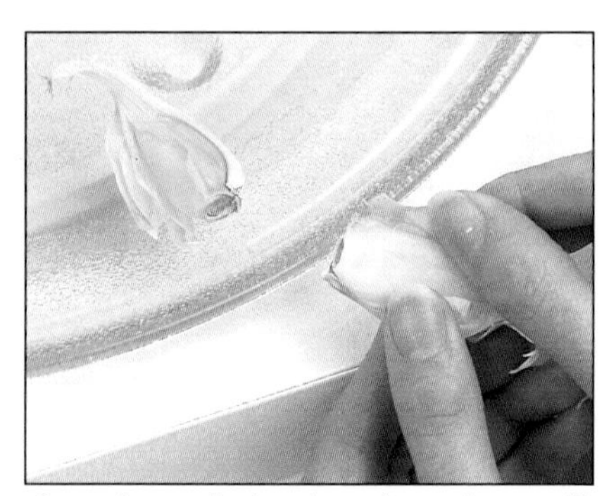

Once the garlic has been heated you will find the outer skin peels away easily.

HEATING TACO SHELLS

Place taco shells on a microwave-safe plate, openings facing downwards. Heat for 1 minute on High (100%).

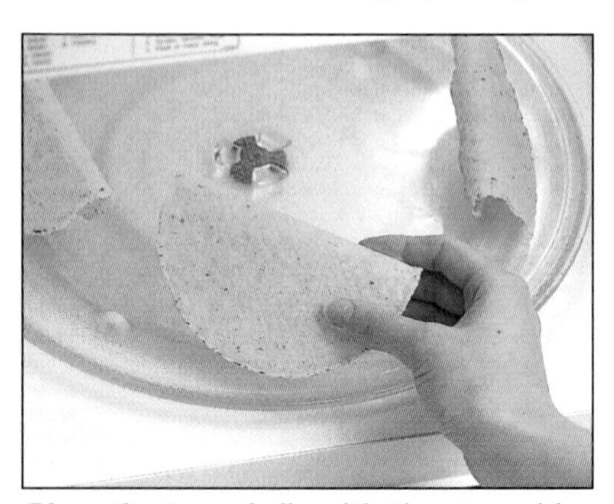

Place the taco shells with the open sides facing downwards.

SCRAMBLED EGGS

Melt 30 g (1 oz) butter in a microwave-safe bowl, add 3 eggs, 1/4 cup (60 ml/2 fl oz) milk and a pinch of salt. Whisk together with a fork. Cook on High (100%) for 1 minute, remove from microwave and stir well with a fork. Cook for a further 30 seconds, stir again, then cook for 20 seconds and stir again. Leave to stand for 1–2 minutes before serving, as the egg will continue cooking.

Whisk together the melted butter, eggs, milk and a pinch of salt.

It is important to stir the egg regularly during cooking.

DISSOLVING GELATINE

Place the liquid (usually water or fruit juice, depending on your recipe) in a small bowl. Sprinkle the gelatine over, but do not stir. Heat on High (100%) for 30 seconds, then stir with a fork until dissolved.

Sprinkle the gelatine over the liquid but do not stir.

Stir with a fork after cooking to check the gelatine is fully dissolved.

CLARIFIED BUTTER

Melt butter in a microwave-safe jug on High (100%) until foaming. Set aside for a few minutes, then skim the froth from the surface and discard. Pour the liquid butter into a bowl, avoiding the milky white whey.

Set aside for a few minutes and then skim the froth from the surface.

Pour the liquid 'clarified' butter into a bowl, avoiding the whey at the bottom.

COOKING BACON

Place 3–4 rashers bacon in a single layer between sheets of paper towel. Cook on High (100%) for 3 minutes, or longer if you prefer your bacon crispy.

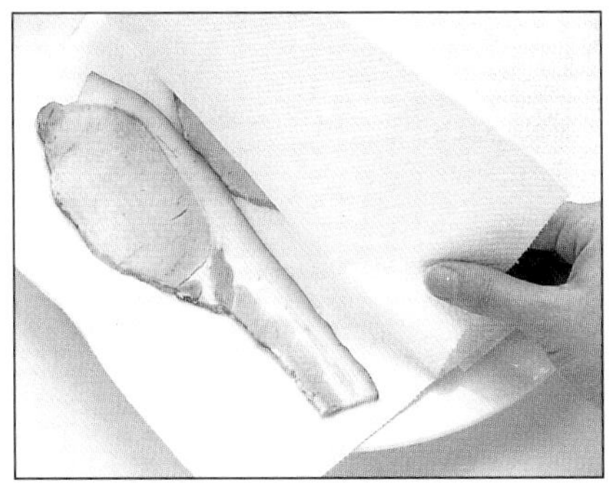

Cook the bacon in paper towel to prevent it spitting, and absorb the fat.

MAKING POPPADOMS

Put 2–3 poppadoms on glasses around the turntable and cook on High (100%) for 1 minute, or until puffed.

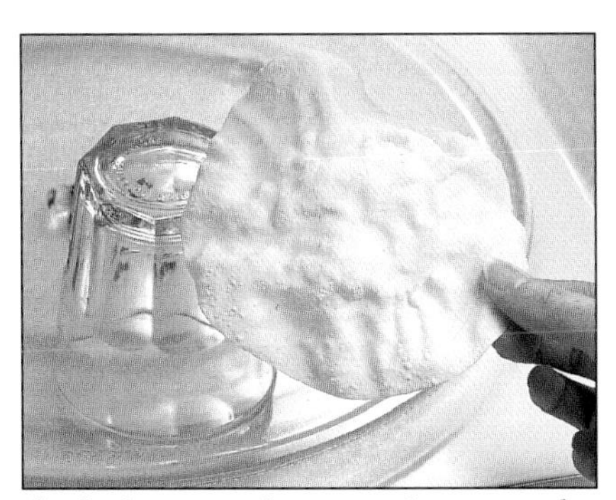

Cook the poppadoms on glasses so the microwaves can heat them from all sides.

JUICY FRUIT

Prick a whole lemon, lime or orange with a fork. Heat on High (100%) for 1 minute to produce more juice.

Prick the fruit with a fork so it doesn't burst in the microwave.

MAKING CROUTONS

Melt a little butter in a bowl in the microwave. Remove the crusts from slices of bread and brush lightly with the butter. Cut into small cubes and put on a microwave-safe plate. Cook in 1 minute bursts on High (100%) until crisp and golden.

Remove the crusts from slices of bread and brush with melted butter.

Cook the croutons in 1 minute bursts until crisp and golden.

DRIED HERBS

Strip the leaves from the stems and spread in a single layer between two sheets of paper towel. Place on the microwave turntable and cook in 1 minute bursts on High (100%), until the leaves are crisp and dry. Store in an airtight container.

Place the leaves between layers of paper towel to absorb any moisture.

Once the leaves are dry and crisp they will crumble easily.

DRYING CITRUS PEEL

Using a vegetable peeler or small sharp knife, peel strips of rind from citrus fruit, avoiding the white pith. Spread out onto a microwave-safe plate and cook in 1 minute bursts on High (100%), until the peel is dried and just crisp on the edges. Keep in an airtight container and use to flavour dishes whenever fresh peel is required.

Cut away the white pith from the strips of peel to avoid bitterness.

Cook in 1 minute bursts until the peel is dried and just crisp at the edges.

SOUPS AND STARTERS

MINESTRONE

Preparation time: 25 minutes
Total cooking time: 40 minutes
Serves 6

1/2 cup (80 g/2 2/3 oz) small macaroni
2 tablespoons vegetable oil
1 onion, chopped
1 clove garlic, chopped
2 rashers bacon, chopped
1 carrot, chopped
1 potato, chopped
1 celery stick, chopped
1 zucchini, sliced
100 g (3 1/3 oz) green beans, cut into short lengths
425 g (13 1/2 oz) can chopped tomatoes
300 g (9 2/3 oz) can four-bean mix, rinsed and drained
3 cups (750 ml/24 fl oz) vegetable stock
1/4 teaspoon dried thyme leaves
1/2 cup (50 g/1 2/3 oz) freshly grated Parmesan

1 Place the pasta in a microwave-safe bowl and pour boiling water over until well covered. Cook on High (100%) for 8 minutes, or until tender. Drain well in a colander, then transfer to a bowl. Toss with 1 tablespoon of the oil to prevent the pasta sticking together and set aside until needed.
2 Combine the remaining oil, onion, garlic and bacon in a large (about 14-cup/3 1/2 litre capacity) microwave-safe bowl. Cover with paper towels; cook on High (100%) for 3 minutes.
3 Add the carrot, potato, celery, zucchini, beans, tomatoes, canned beans, stock, thyme and 3 cups (750 ml/24 fl oz) water and mix well. Cook on High (100%) for 25 minutes, stirring occasionally.
4 Stir in the cooked macaroni and season well with salt and pepper. Reheat on High (100%) for 3 minutes. Spoon into serving bowls, sprinkle with grated Parmesan cheese and serve with crusty bread.

COOK'S FILE

Note: Four-bean mix is a canned mixture of kidney, butter, baby lima beans and chickpeas. If it is not available, use a 300 g (9 2/3 oz) can of kidney beans instead.
Hint: When microwaving, we cover dishes with paper towels just to stop any oil or fat spitting.

Put the oil, onion, garlic and bacon in a large bowl and cover with paper towel.

Once the soup is cooked, stir in the pasta and season to taste.

WARM SEAFOOD SALAD

Preparation time: 20 minutes
Total cooking time: 5 minutes
Serves 4

12 raw prawns, peeled and deveined, tails left intact
12 scallops
200 g (6½ oz) white fish fillets, cut into short, thin strips
1 tablespoon fresh lemon juice
12 black mussels (see note)
4 tablespoons olive oil
2 tablespoons white wine vinegar
½ teaspoon sugar
1 small clove garlic, crushed
⅓ cup (20 g/⅔ oz) chopped fresh parsley
mixed lettuce leaves, to serve

1 Place the prawns, scallops and fish in a microwave-safe dish, sprinkle with lemon juice and cook, covered, on High (100%) for 3 minutes. Drain and then leave to rest for 3 minutes.

2 Scrub the mussels, discarding the beards, and put in a microwave-safe bowl. Cover and cook for 2 minutes on High (100%). Discard any unopened mussels, drain and add to the seafood.

3 Whisk the oil, vinegar, sugar, garlic and parsley, season to taste and pour over the warm seafood. Toss gently. Place the lettuce leaves on a plate and top with warm seafood.

COOK'S FILE

Note: Only buy mussels which are tightly closed. Open ones are dead.

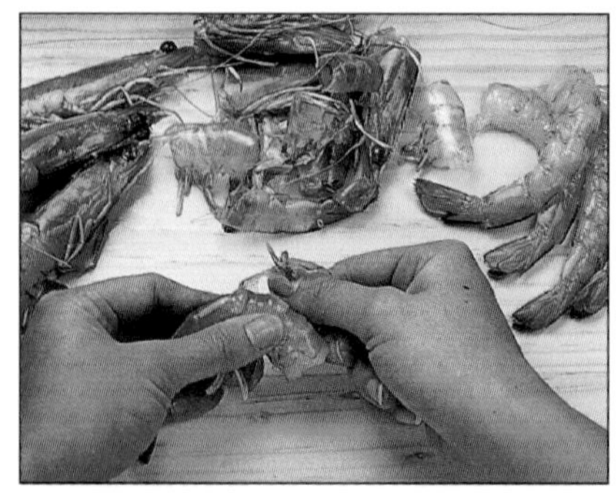

Peel and devein the prawns, removing the heads but leaving the tails intact.

Cook the mussels for 2 minutes and then discard any that haven't opened.

Mix together the dressing ingredients and then pour over the warm seafood.

PRAWN PATE

Preparation time: 15 minutes + chilling
Total cooking time: 2 minutes
Serves 4–6

750 g/1½ lb raw prawns, peeled and deveined
2 tablespoons lemon juice
75 g (2½ oz) unsalted butter
1 tablespoon mayonnaise
pinch of ground nutmeg
1 clove garlic, crushed
½ teaspoon Tabasco

1 Place the prawns in a microwave-safe dish and sprinkle with 1 tablespoon lemon juice. Cover loosely and cook on High (100%) for 1 minute 30 seconds. Leave to cool slightly.
2 Put the butter in a food processor and process to soften. Add the prawns and juice, mayonnaise, nutmeg, garlic, Tabasco and remaining lemon juice. Process until smooth.
3 Spoon into a serving dish and place in the refrigerator for at least 1 hour before serving.

COOK'S FILE

Note: Freshly ground whole nutmeg will give the best flavour.

Sprinkle one tablespoon of lemon juice over the raw prawns.

Add the prawns, lemon juice, garlic, mayonnaise and Tabasco to the butter.

Spoon the paté into a serving dish before refrigerating for 1 hour.

STUFFED MUSHROOMS

Preparation time: 20 minutes
Total cooking time: 10 minutes
Serves 4

8 cup mushrooms
1 tablespoon olive oil
1 onion, finely chopped
1 clove garlic, crushed
2 rashers bacon, chopped
3 tablespoons fresh breadcrumbs
1 tablespoon chopped fresh parsley
1/2 cup (50 g/1 2/3 oz) freshly grated Parmesan
lemon pepper, to taste

1 Peel and discard the skin from the mushrooms. Remove the stems and chop roughly, reserving the caps. In a microwave-safe bowl, mix the stems with the oil, onion, garlic and bacon and cover with paper towels. Cook on High (100%) for 4 minutes.

2 Mix in the breadcrumbs, parsley and half the Parmesan cheese and then season well with lemon pepper.

3 Spoon into the mushroom caps. Place in an oiled heatproof and microwave-safe dish and cook on High (100%) for 4 minutes. Sprinkle the remaining Parmesan cheese over the top of the mushrooms and place under a preheated grill until golden.

COOK'S FILE

Note: For a vegetarian version, replace the bacon with 2 tablespoons chopped black olives.

Peel the mushrooms, discarding the skin, and then remove the stems.

Mix in the breadcrumbs, parsley and half the Parmesan, then season.

Place the mushrooms in an oiled dish, then sprinkle with the remaining cheese.

BROCCOLI SOUP

Preparation time: 20 minutes
Total cooking time: 24 minutes
Serves 4

30 g (1 oz) butter
1 onion, finely chopped
500 g (1 lb) broccoli
2 cups (500 ml/16 fl oz) chicken stock
1 cup (250 ml/8 fl oz) cream

1 Melt the butter in a microwave-safe bowl on High (100%) for 30 seconds. Add the onion and cook on High (100%) for 3 minutes. Cut the florets from the broccoli stalks and set aside. Roughly chop the stalks and add to the onion with the stock. Cover and cook on High (100%) for 5 minutes.
2 Stir in the florets and cook, uncovered, for 10 minutes. Season with salt and pepper. Cool slightly.
3 Place the soup into a food processor and process until smooth. Add the cream and process briefly. Reheat on Medium (50%) for 5 minutes, stirring after every minute.

The broccoli stalks will take longer to cook than the florets.

Cook the stalks in the stock for 5 minutes then add the florets.

Process the soup until smooth, then add the cream and process briefly.

BABA GHANOUJ

Preparation time: 10 minutes
Total cooking time: 5 minutes
Serves 4

1 eggplant (about 500 g/1 lb)
1 clove garlic, crushed
2 tablespoons lemon juice
1/4 cup (70 g/2 1/3 oz) tahini
1 teaspoon ground cumin
1/2 teaspoon paprika

1 Cut the stalk off the eggplant and prick the skin a few times with a sharp knife to prevent bursting.
2 Put the whole eggplant in a microwave-safe bowl, cover loosely with plastic wrap and cook on High (100%) for 5 minutes.
3 Leave the eggplant until cool enough to handle and then scoop out the soft flesh into a food processor. Add the remaining ingredients and process until reasonably smooth. Season to taste with salt and pepper. Serve with warm pitta bread.

COOK'S FILE

Note: Tahini is a paste made from sesame seeds, available from health food shops or some supermarkets.

Cut the stalk off the eggplant and pierce the skin several times with a sharp knife.

Put the eggplant in a bowl and cover loosely with plastic wrap.

Process the eggplant, garlic, lemon juice, tahini, cumin, paprika and seasonings.

Rinse the vine leaves under cold running water and then leave to soak.

Stir in the rice, dill, mint, lemon rind, lemon juice and pine nuts.

Place 2 teaspoons of filling at the stem end of the leaf and roll up into a parcel.

Arrange the stuffed vine leaves in one layer in the dish and pour over the water.

DOLMADES (Stuffed Vine Leaves)

Preparation time: 45 minutes
Total cooking time: 28 minutes
Serves 4–6

200 g (6½ oz) vine leaves
⅓ cup (80 ml/2¾ fl oz) olive oil
2 onions, finely chopped
2 cloves garlic, crushed
¾ cup (165 g/5½ oz) short-grain rice
3 tablespoons chopped fresh dill
1 tablespoon chopped fresh mint
2 teaspoons finely grated lemon rind
2 tablespoons lemon juice
3 tablespoons pine nuts
2 tablespoons extra virgin olive oil

1 Rinse the leaves under cold water; soak while preparing the filling.

2 Heat the oil in a microwave-safe bowl on High (100%) for 3 minutes. Add the onion and garlic and cook on High (100%) for 3 minutes. Stir in the rice, dill, mint, lemon rind, 1 tablespoon lemon juice and the pine nuts. Cover tightly and cook on High (100%) for 5 minutes. Uncover, season with salt and pepper and leave to cool.

3 Lay out the vine leaves on the work surface, vein-side-up and with the stem closest to you. Place 2 teaspoons of rice mixture at the stem end. Roll up towards the tip of the leaf, folding in the sides as you go. Repeat with the remaining leaves and filling.

4 Arrange the stuffed leaves in a single layer in a large microwave-safe dish. Pour 2 cups (500 ml/16 fl oz) water over the vine leaves, cover tightly and cook on High (100%) for 17 minutes. Leave for 5–10 minutes before serving. To serve, combine the remaining lemon juice and olive oil and pour over the Dolmades.

COOK'S FILE

Note: Vine leaves are available in brine, either in packets or tins, from most delicatessens.

CARROT SOUP

Preparation time: 15 minutes
Total cooking time: 18 minutes
Serves 4

30 g (1 oz) butter
1 onion, chopped
500 g (1 lb) carrots, peeled and roughly chopped
2 teaspoons ground cumin
2½ cups (600 ml/20 fl oz) chicken stock
300 ml (9½ fl oz) cream
1 tablespoon chopped chives, to garnish

1 Melt the butter in a microwave-safe bowl for 30 seconds on High (100%). Stir in the chopped onion and cook for 2 minutes on High (100%).
2 Stir through the carrot and cumin, cover loosely and cook for 4 minutes on High (100%). Add 1 cup (250 ml/ 8 fl oz) of the stock, stir well and cook for a further 7 minutes. Allow to cool a little before processing.
3 Put the soup in a food processor and process until very smooth, adding the remaining stock and 1 cup (250 ml/8 fl oz) of the cream while the motor is running. Add salt and freshly ground black pepper to taste and reheat for about 4 minutes on Medium (50%). Swirl in the remaining cream and scatter with the chopped chives to serve.

COOK'S FILE

Variation: If you prefer not to use cream, add an extra cup (250 ml/ 8 fl oz) of stock instead. Ready-made stock is very convenient but can be rather salty—try diluting it half and half with water.

Melt the butter and then add the onion and cook for 2 minutes.

Cook the carrot and cumin, then add a cup of stock and cook for 7 minutes.

Process the soup in a food processor, adding the cream and remaining stock.

OYSTERS MORNAY

Preparation time: 10 minutes
Total cooking time: 7 minutes
Serves 6

18 fresh oysters in their shells
20 g (2/3 oz) butter
1 tablespoon plain flour
1 cup (250 ml/8 fl oz) milk
3/4 cup (90 g/3 oz) grated Cheddar cheese
1/2 cup (50 g/1 2/3) freshly grated Parmesan

1 Remove any grit from the oysters with paper towels. Melt the butter in a microwave bowl on High (100%) for 30 seconds. Stir in the flour and cook on High (100%) for 1 minute. Whisk in the milk and cook on High (100%) for 4 minutes; whisk every minute.
2 Add the cheeses and season well with black pepper. Stir until the cheese has melted and the mixture is smooth. Spoon 2–3 teaspoonsful of the mixture into each oyster shell.
3 Place the oysters around the edge of a microwave-safe plate and cook on High (100%) for 40 seconds, or until they are just heated through.

Use paper towel to remove any grit from the oysters.

Melt the butter, then stir in the flour and cook for 1 minute. Whisk in the milk.

Add the Cheddar and Parmesan cheeses and stir until melted.

Spoon the cheese mixture into the shells then place round the edge of a plate.

COOK'S FILE

Variation: Sprinkle with extra grated cheese and place under a preheated grill until golden brown.

SPICY POTATO WEDGES

Preparation time: 20 minutes
Total cooking time: 12 minutes
Serves 4

500 g (1 lb) potatoes
2 tablespoons olive oil
2 tablespoons Cajun seasoning
2 teaspoons garlic powder
2 tablespoons chopped chives
2/3 cup (160 g/5 1/4 oz) sour cream

1 Wash the potatoes and dry well with paper towels to ensure a crisp finish. Cut each potato into 2 cm (3/4 inch) wedges and brush all over with the olive oil.
2 Mix together the Cajun seasoning and garlic powder and spread out onto a sheet of paper towel. Lightly roll each wedge in the seasoning mix, shaking off any excess.
3 Arrange the wedges, skin-side-down, on sheets of paper towel on the microwave turntable. Cook on High (100%) for 12 minutes. In a bowl, mix together the chives and sour cream to make a serving dip.

COOK'S FILE

Note: Wedges make a great snack, or accompaniment to barbecued meats.
Variation: Serve sweet chilli sauce alongside the sour cream dip.
Note: Cajun seasoning is a mixture of spices, available in jars from most supermarkets or from speciality gourmet shops.

Cut the unpeeled potatoes into thick wedges and brush with oil.

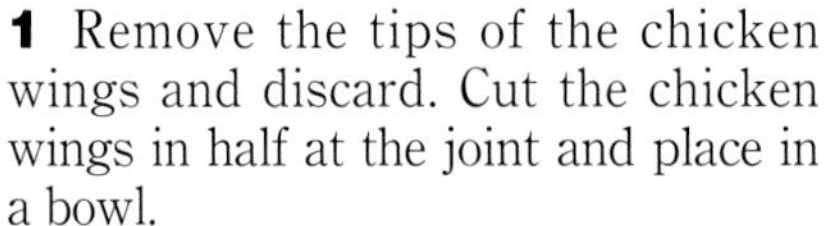

Mix together the seasoning and garlic powder and lightly coat the potato.

Arrange the wedges, skin-side-down, around the outside of the turntable.

CHICKEN WINGS IN HONEY AND GINGER

Preparation time: 30 minutes + 1 hour marinating
Total cooking time: 11 minutes
Serves 4–6

6 chicken wings
1/3 cup (80 ml/2 3/4 fl oz) soy sauce
2 teaspoons honey
1 clove garlic, crushed
1 teaspoon grated fresh ginger
1 tablespoon dry sherry
toasted sesame seeds, to garnish

1 Remove the tips of the chicken wings and discard. Cut the chicken wings in half at the joint and place in a bowl.
2 Put the soy sauce, honey, garlic, ginger and sherry in a small bowl and mix well. Pour over the chicken wings, cover and refrigerate for at least 1 hour, stirring once or twice during marinating.
3 Arrange the wings in a single layer in a microwave-safe casserole dish, pour over half the marinade to thoroughly coat the chicken, then cook on High (100%) for 6 minutes. Turn the chicken wings over and rearrange to ensure even cooking. Pour over the remaining marinade. Cook on High (100%) for a further 5 minutes. Leave for 4–5 minutes before serving. Place the wings on a plate and sprinkle with the toasted sesame seeds.

COOK'S FILE

Variation: To make a serving sauce, place the marinade in a frying pan, bring to the boil, then reduce the heat and simmer until reduced by half; serve over the wings. Alternatively, make a tangy dipping sauce by combining 1 cup (250 ml/8 fl oz) yoghurt with 1 teaspoon lime juice cordial and a little chopped mint.

Use a pair of scissors to cut the chicken wings in half at the joint.

Mix together the soy sauce, honey, garlic, ginger and sherry to make a marinade.

Turn and rearrange the chicken wings to ensure they cook evenly.

Spicy Potato Wedges (top) and Chicken Wings in Honey and Ginger

PUMPKIN SOUP

Preparation time: 10 minutes
Total cooking time: 17 minutes
Serves 2

500 g (1 lb) pumpkin
1/2 teaspoon ground cumin
1 1/2 cups (375 ml/12 fl oz) hot chicken stock
1/4 cup (60 ml/2 fl oz) cream
1 tablespoon fresh herbs

1 Peel and chop the pumpkin into chunks and put in a large microwave-safe bowl with the cumin and hot chicken stock.
2 Cover loosely and cook on High (100%) for 15 minutes, or until the pumpkin is tender.
3 Leave to cool, then process until smooth in a food processor. Stir through the cream and reheat on Medium (50%) for 1–2 minutes, or until heated through. Scatter with herbs and black pepper to serve.

COOK'S FILE

Hint: To make pumpkin easier to peel, put it in the microwave and cook on High (100%) for 2 minutes. Leave to soften for 1 minute, then peel.

Peel the pumpkin and chop into even-sized chunks.

Cook the pumpkin in stock until tender. Test it with a sharp knife.

Put the pumpkin and cooking liquid in a food processor and mix until smooth.

SPICY BEAN SOUP

Preparation time: 15 minutes
Total cooking time: 1 hour 15 minutes
Serves 4

3 tablespoons dried black-eyed beans
3 tablespoons dried red kidney beans
3 tablespoons dried pinto beans
3 tablespoons dried haricot beans
1 tablespoon oil
1 leek, chopped
2 cloves garlic, chopped
1 stick celery, chopped
1 carrot, chopped
425 g (13½ oz) can chopped tomatoes
1 tablespoon thyme leaves
½–1 teaspoon chilli powder
1 bay leaf
2 cups (500 ml/16 fl oz) vegetable stock

1 Place the beans in a microwave-safe bowl and cover with boiling water. Cover and cook on High (100%) for 40 minutes; stir every 10 minutes. Leave for 5–10 minutes, then drain and set aside.

2 Put the oil, leek and garlic in a microwave-safe bowl and cook on High (100%) for 3 minutes. Stir in the celery and carrot; cook for 2 minutes. Stir in the tomatoes, thyme, chilli powder, bay leaf, stock and 2 cups (500 ml/16 fl oz) water.

3 Mix in the beans. Cover and cook on High (100%) for 30 minutes; stir every 10 minutes. Leave to stand for 5–10 minutes, before serving with crusty bread.

Put the beans in a bowl, cover with boiling water and cook for 40 minutes.

Cook the leek and garlic in the oil, then add the celery and carrot.

Stir in the drained beans, cover and cook for 30 minutes.

CHICKEN LIVER PATE

Preparation time: 10 minutes + 1 hour chilling
Total cooking time: 7 minutes
Serves 4

100 g ($3^1/_3$ oz) butter
$^1/_2$ small onion, chopped
2 cloves garlic, crushed
250 g (8 oz) chicken livers, rinsed and any membrane removed, chopped
2 tablespoons port or brandy

1 Melt the butter in a microwave-safe bowl for 1 minute on High (100%). Stir in the onion and garlic and cook on High (100%) for 3 minutes.

2 Add the chicken livers and stir well, so that they are coated with the butter mixture. Cover loosely and cook on High (100%) for 1 minute and then on Medium (50%) for 2 minutes. Leave to cool.

3 Put the mixture in a food processor and add the port or brandy. Process until smooth, season with salt and black pepper and then pour into a serving dish, smoothing the surface. Refrigerate for at least 1 hour before serving, to allow the pâté to set.

Melt the butter, then cook the onion and garlic for 3 minutes.

Add the chicken livers and stir well so that they are coated with butter.

Process the mixture until smooth and then pour into a serving dish.

TOMATO AND LENTIL SOUP

Preparation time: 15 minutes
Total cooking time: 19 minutes
Serves 4

1 onion, roughly chopped
1 tablespoon olive oil
2 cloves garlic, crushed
410 g (13 oz) can crushed tomatoes
1/2 cup (125 g/4 oz) red lentils
2 cups (500 ml/16 fl oz) chicken stock
pinch of cayenne pepper or chilli powder (optional)
juice of 1 orange
100 g (3 1/3 oz) plain yoghurt and chopped chives, to garnish

1 Put the onion, oil and garlic in a large microwave-safe bowl and cook for 2 minutes on High (100%). Add the tomato, lentils, stock and cayenne or chilli powder. Cook on High (100%) for 15 minutes and then leave to cool.
2 Purée in a food processor until very smooth and then add the orange juice and salt and pepper to taste.
3 Reheat on High (100%) when ready to serve. Garnish with a swirl of yoghurt and some chopped chives.

COOK'S FILE

Note: If good-quality fresh tomatoes are available, use 3 peeled and chopped tomatoes instead of the can.

Add the tomatoes, stock, cayenne or chilli powder and red lentils.

To prevent hot splashes, allow the soup mixture to cool before puréeing.

Purée the soup until smooth and then add the orange juice.

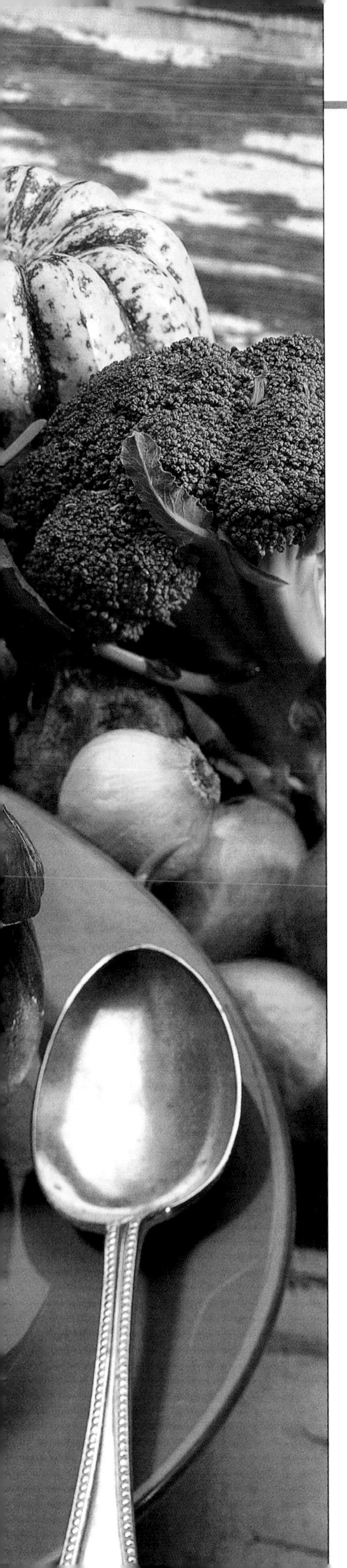

VEGETABLE ASIDES

STUFFED NUGGET PUMPKINS

Preparation time: 30 minutes
Total cooking time: 25 minutes
Serves 4

4 nugget pumpkins
30 g (1 oz) butter
1 small leek, sliced
1 clove garlic, crushed
2 teaspoons ground cumin
1 teaspoon garam masala
1 stick celery, chopped
1 small zucchini, chopped
1 tomato, chopped
100 g (3 1/3 oz) button mushrooms, chopped
1/2 cup (90 g/3 oz) cooked short-grain rice
1/4 cup (40 g/1 1/3 oz) toasted pine nuts
1/2 cup (60 g/2 oz) grated Cheddar cheese

1 Slice the top from each pumpkin and set aside. Using a spoon, scoop out the seeds and discard.
2 Place the pumpkin shells and lids in a heatproof and microwave-safe dish, pour in 3 tablespoons water, cover and cook on High (100%) for 10 minutes. Remove the pumpkins and leave upside-down to drain.
3 Melt the butter in a microwave-safe bowl on High (100%) for 30 seconds; stir in the leek and garlic and cook on High (100%) for 3 minutes. Mix in the cumin and garam masala and cook for 2 minutes. Add the celery, zucchini, tomato and mushrooms and cook on High (100%) for 5 minutes. Stir in the rice and pine nuts. Season well.
4 Spoon into the pumpkin shells, place in the cleaned dish and cook on High (100%) for 4 minutes. Sprinkle with cheese and place under a pre-heated grill until melted. Replace the lids to serve, if preferred.

COOK'S FILE

Note: To make your own garam masala, put 4 tablespoons coriander seeds, 3 tablespoons cardamom pods, 1 tablespoon whole black peppercorns, 2 tablespoons cumin seeds, 1 teaspoon whole cloves and 3 cinnamon sticks in a small pan. Dry-fry over moderate heat until fragrant. Peel the cardamom pods, retaining the seeds only. Put the spices in a blender or processor with a grated whole fresh nutmeg and grind into a powder. Store in an airtight jar.

Cut the tops off the pumpkins and then scoop out the seeds and discard.

Cook the spices and vegetables in butter, then add the rice and pine nuts.

JACKET POTATOES

Preparation time: 7 minutes
Total cooking time: 10 minutes
Serves 2

2 large red-skinned potatoes
1 tablespoon olive oil
butter or sour cream and chopped chives, to serve

1 Scrub the potatoes thoroughly and dry with paper towels. Prick all over with a fork. (It is important to do this or the potato skins will burst open during cooking.)
2 Rub olive oil into the potato skins, then sprinkle generously with salt. Wrap in a couple of sheets of paper towel and place around the outside of the microwave turntable.
3 Cook the potatoes on High (100%) for 10 minutes; turn after 5 minutes. Leave for 5 minutes before serving.
4 To serve, cut a cross in the top of each potato and squeeze the sides with a finger and thumb, so that the cross opens up. Fill with butter or sour cream and top with fresh chives.

COOK'S FILE

Note: Old potatoes, such as Pontiac or Desirée, are best for baking.

Prick the potatoes all over with a fork to prevent them bursting.

The paper towel will absorb any moisture and give the potatoes a crisp finish.

Squeeze the potato to open it up and give a good space for filling.

VEGETABLE PUREES

Preparation time: 20 minutes
Total cooking time: 17 minutes
Serves 4

Celeriac Purée
1 large (about 750 g/1½ lb) celeriac
30 g (1 oz) soft butter
1 tablespoon chopped coriander leaves

Sweet Potato Purée
750 g (1½ lb) sweet potato
½ cup (125 ml/4 fl oz) vegetable stock
1½ teaspoons ground cumin
30 g (1 oz) soft butter

1 To make Celeriac Purée: Cut the celeriac into quarters, then peel and chop. Place in a microwave-safe bowl and sprinkle with 2 tablespoons water. Cover tightly and cook on High (100%) for 9 minutes. Cool slightly.

2 Place in a food processor with the butter and process until smooth. Season well with salt and pepper and fold through the coriander.

3 To make Sweet Potato Purée: Peel and chop the sweet potato and place in a microwave-safe bowl with the vegetable stock and cumin. Cover tightly and cook on High (100%) for 8 minutes. Cool slightly, then put in a food processor with the butter, season to taste with salt and pepper and process until smooth.

Cut the celeriac into quarters, then peel and cut into cubes.

Put the chopped sweet potato in a bowl with the stock and cumin.

Process the cooked sweet potato with the butter and salt and pepper, to taste.

RATATOUILLE

Preparation time: 20 minutes
Total cooking time: 12 minutes
Serves 4

4 ripe tomatoes
2 slender eggplants, thickly sliced
1 onion, roughly chopped into wedges
2 zucchini, thickly sliced
1/2 red capsicum, seeded and chopped
1 tablespoon tomato paste
2 cloves garlic, crushed
3 tablespoons olive oil
1 teaspoon sugar
1 tablespoon red wine vinegar
1/2 teaspoon thyme leaves
2 tablespoons finely chopped fresh parsley

1 Skin the tomatoes by scoring a cross in the base of each and then immersing them in boiling water for 1 minute. Lift out, plunge in cold water and peel away the skin from the cross. Chop the tomato flesh.

2 Put the tomato with the remaining ingredients, except the parsley, in a large microwave-safe bowl. Stir well, cover and cook for 12 minutes on High (100%), stirring every 4 minutes.

3 Leave to rest for at least 10 minutes before serving, longer if possible, to allow the flavours to develop. Season with salt and black pepper. Scatter with the chopped parsley.

COOK'S FILE

Variation: If fresh tomatoes are not at their best, use a 410 g/13 oz can of chopped tomatoes.

Hint: It is not necessary to salt slender eggplants before use as they are not as bitter as the large ones.

Thickly slice the eggplants and zucchini and chop the capsicum.

Plunge the tomatoes into boiling water, then cold, and peel away the skin.

Stir together all the ingredients except the parsley, and cook for 12 minutes.

CAULIFLOWER AU GRATIN

Preparation time: 15 minutes
Total cooking time: 16 minutes
Serves 4

30 g (1 oz) butter
1 tablespoon plain flour
1 cup (250 ml/8 fl oz) milk
1/2 cup (125 g/4 oz) grated Cheddar cheese
1/2 cauliflower, cut into florets

Crumb Topping
30 g (1 oz) butter
1 cup (80 g/2 2/3 oz) fresh white breadcrumbs
3 tablespoons chopped parsley

1 Melt the butter in a microwave-safe bowl for 30 seconds on High (100%). Whisk in the flour and then cook for 20 seconds on High (100%).
2 Whisk in the milk gradually until well combined and then cook on High (100%) for 4 minutes, whisking after 2 minutes. Stir in the grated cheese and set aside.
3 Put the cauliflower florets in a microwave-safe dish, cover and cook for 5 minutes on High (100%). Pour the cheese sauce over the cooked cauliflower and reheat for 1 minute on High (100%).
4 To make Crumb Topping: In a frying pan melt the butter and add the breadcrumbs. Cook until golden. Sprinkle the crumbs and parsley over the cauliflower and serve.

Melt the butter, then whisk in the flour and cook for 20 seconds.

Add the milk and cook for 4 minutes, whisking after 2 minutes.

Cover the cauliflower and cook—you don't need to add any water.

Melt the butter in a frying pan and cook the breadcrumbs until golden.

COOK'S FILE

Note: This recipe also works nicely with broccoli florets or a mixture of both broccoli and cauliflower.

GLAZED BABY BEETROOT

Preparation time: 15 minutes
Total cooking time: 17 minutes
Serves 4

12 baby beetroots
20 g (2/3 oz) butter
1 onion, sliced
1/2 cup (125 ml/4 fl oz) orange juice
1 teaspoon grated orange rind
1 tablespoon soft brown sugar

1 Cut the leaves off the beetroots, leaving a little stalk. Pierce the beetroots once or twice with a fork. Place in a shallow microwave-safe dish, pour over 3 tablespoons water, then cover and cook on High (100%) for 10 minutes. Allow to cool slightly.
2 While the beetroots are still warm, trim the roots, then slip the skins off the beetroots.
3 Melt the butter in a microwave-safe bowl on High (100%) for 30 seconds. Add the onion and cook for 2 minutes on High (100%). Mix in the orange juice, orange rind and sugar and cook on High (100%) for 2 minutes. Stir in the baby beetroot and cook for a further 2 minutes. Leave to stand for a few minutes before serving.

COOK'S FILE

Note: Try to choose even-sized beetroots that will cook evenly. It may be a good idea to wear latex gloves when handling beetroot, as the juice can stain your hands. For this recipe we pierce the beetroots, to stop them bursting in the microwave. Normally, you wouldn't pierce beetroots as they tend to bleed.

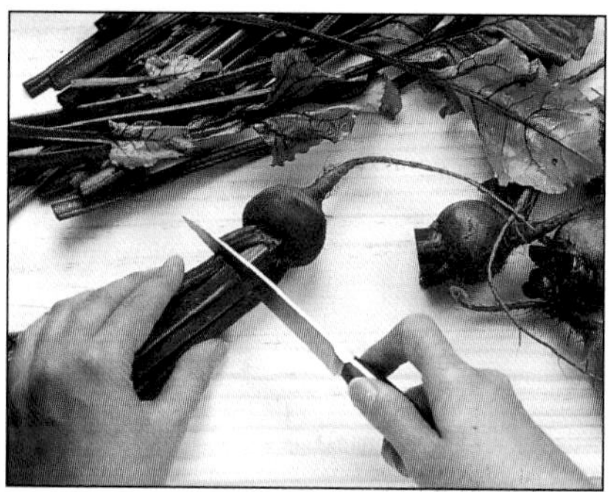

Trim the leaves from the baby beetroots, leaving a small amount of stalk.

Trim the tops and roots from the beetroots and slip off the skins.

Stir the beetroots into the onion and orange mixture.

LAYERED VEGETABLE BAKE

Preparation time: 25 minutes
Total cooking time: 34 minutes
Serves 4

30 g (1 oz) butter
1 leek, sliced
2 potatoes
500 g (1 lb) pumpkin
350 g (11 1/4 oz) sweet potato
3/4 cup (90 g/3 oz) grated Cheddar cheese
3/4 cup (185 ml/6 fl oz) cream
ground nutmeg

1 Melt the butter in a microwave-safe bowl on High (100%) for 30 seconds, stir in the leek and cook on High (100%) for 3 minutes. Meanwhile, peel and thinly slice the potatoes, pumpkin and sweet potato.
2 In a 6-cup (1.5 litre) microwave-safe dish, layer slices of potato, pumpkin, leek and sweet potato, finishing with a layer of sweet potato.
3 Sprinkle over the cheese and pour cream over the top. Sprinkle with ground nutmeg and black pepper, to taste, and cook on Medium (50%) for 30 minutes.

COOK'S FILE

Note: If you want to brown the top of this dish, you can flash it under a hot grill for a few minutes just before serving. Ideally, it is best to buy whole fresh spices and prepare them yourself. Nutmeg can be bought whole and grated as required—the flavour is far superior to that of ready-ground nutmeg in packets, as is the case with all spices.

Peel and thinly slice the potato, pumpkin and sweet potato,

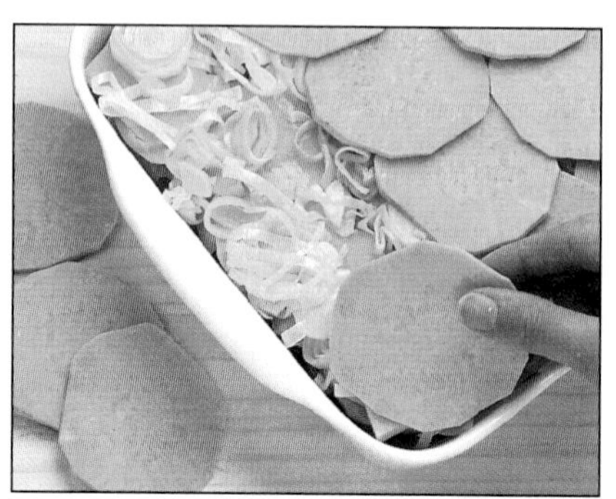

Layer slices of potato, pumpkin, leek and sweet potato in the dish.

Top with cheese, pour over the cream, then sprinkle with pepper and nutmeg.

Glazed Baby Beetroot (top) and Layered Vegetable Bake

CARAMELISED ONIONS

Preparation time: 10 minutes
Total cooking time: 13 minutes
Serves 4

4 medium onions
50 g (1⅔ oz) butter
2 tablespoons soft brown sugar

1 Peel the onions and cut in half horizontally. Place in a shallow microwave-safe dish in a single layer.
2 Combine the butter and sugar in a microwave-safe bowl and cook on High (100%) for 1 minute. Mix well and spoon over the onions. Spread evenly with the back of the spoon. Cover and cook on High (100%) for 6 minutes.
3 Baste the onions with the butter mixture, then re-cover and cook for a further 6 minutes on High (100%). Spoon the butter mixture over the top and sprinkle with chopped fresh parsley to serve.

COOK'S FILE

Note: This is a wonderful side dish for serving with meat.

Peel the onions and halve horizontally so they keep their shape.

Cook the butter and sugar, spoon over the onions and spread evenly.

During cooking, baste the onions with the caramelised butter mixture.

POTATO AND OLIVE GALETTE

Preparation time: 20 minutes
Total cooking time: 22 minutes
Serves 4

1 tablespoon olive oil
1 leek, sliced
1 kg (2 lb) potatoes
6 olives, pitted and chopped
2 teaspoons thyme leaves
1/2 cup (125 ml/4 fl oz) chicken stock
1/2 cup (50g/1 2/3 oz) grated Parmesan

1 Place the olive oil and leek in a microwave-safe bowl and cook on High (100%) for 4 minutes.
2 Thinly slice the potatoes and spread a third in a 5-cup (1.25-litre) heatproof and microwave-safe dish. Top with half the leek slices. Sprinkle with olives and then thyme. Repeat the layers, finishing with potato.
3 Pour over the stock, cover and cook on High (100%) for 13 minutes. Sprinkle with Parmesan and season with black pepper. Place under a preheated grill until golden brown.

COOK'S FILE

Note: Ready-made stock can be salty—try using half stock, half water.

Cook the oil and leek in a microwave-safe bowl for 4 minutes.

Layer the potato and leek, then sprinkle with chopped olives and thyme.

Sprinkle with Parmesan and black pepper and brown under a hot grill.

ASPARAGUS WITH WARM VINAIGRETTE

Preparation time: 5 minutes
Total cooking time: 3 minutes
Serves 2

310 g (9 3/4 oz) fresh asparagus
2 teaspoons fresh lemon juice
1 teaspoon finely grated lemon rind
1 tablespoon extra virgin olive oil

1 Wash the asparagus and trim the tough ends from the stems. Place in a single layer in a microwave-safe dish and cover loosely. Cook on High (100%) for 2 minutes 30 seconds.

2 Combine the lemon juice, rind and oil and spoon over the asparagus. Cook on High (100%) for 30 seconds.

3 Sprinkle with salt and cracked black pepper and serve immediately.

COOK'S FILE

Note: Cooking for this length of time keeps the asparagus crunchy. If you prefer it soft cook for a minute longer.

Break off the tough woody ends of the asparagus.

Spoon the oil, lemon juice and lemon rind over the asparagus.

Sprinkle with salt and cracked black pepper and serve immediately.

Mix together the oil, vinegar and crushed garlic and set aside.

Toasting pine nuts in the microwave is easy, but stir them every 2 minutes.

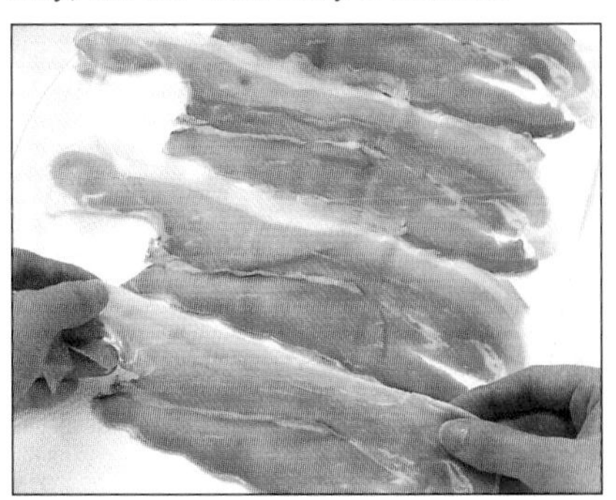

Arrange the prosciutto in a single layer between paper towels.

WARM PASTA SALAD

Preparation time: 20 minutes
Total cooking time: 17 minutes
Serves 4

250 g (8 oz) spiral pasta
3 tablespoons olive oil
1 tablespoon balsamic vinegar
1 clove garlic, crushed
3 tablespoons pine nuts
4 slices prosciutto
60 g (2 oz) sun-dried tomatoes, sliced
50 g (1 2/3 oz) small Italian olives
150 g (4 3/4 oz) rocket leaves, torn

1 Put the pasta in a deep microwave-safe bowl and cover generously with boiling water. Cook on High (100%) for 8 minutes, or until tender. Leave for 5 minutes, drain and set aside. In a jug, mix together the oil, vinegar and garlic and set aside.

2 Put the pine nuts on a microwave-safe plate and cook on High (100%) for 6–7 minutes, or until golden, stirring every 2 minutes. Set aside.

3 Arrange the prosciutto in one layer between paper towels. Cook on High (100%) for 3 minutes, or until crisp. Remove from the paper before it cools and sticks. Crumble the prosciutto.

4 Put the pasta, pine nuts, prosciutto, sun-dried tomatoes, olives and rocket leaves in a serving bowl and toss well. Pour over the dressing and season well with salt and pepper. Serve with crusty bread.

Put the salad ingredients in a bowl and toss together well, then add the dressing.

Quick and Easy Vegetables

A microwave oven really comes into its own when used to cook vegetables. Put the vegetable in a microwave-safe dish with the quantity of water or butter given. Cover with a lid or plastic microwave wrap and cook on High (100%) for the stated time. Because of the speed of cooking, the vegetables retain their colour and nutrients.

BEANS
Quantity: 250 g (8 oz)
Preparation: Top and tail. Add 1–2 tablespoons water.
Cooking time: 3–4 minutes
Serves 4

BRUSSELS SPROUTS
Quantity: 250 g (8 oz)
Preparation: Remove any tough outer leaves and score a cross in the base of each sprout. Add 2 tablespoons water.
Cooking time: 3–4 minutes
Serves 4–6

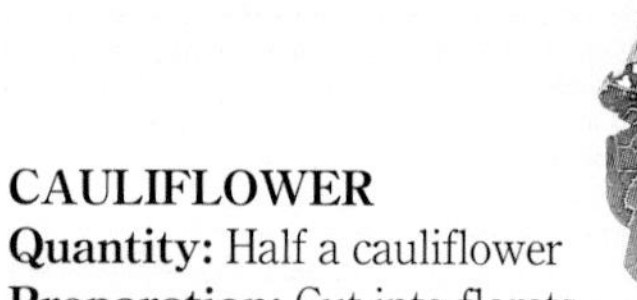

CARROTS
Quantity: 250 g (8 oz)
Preparation: Peel or scrub and cut into slices. Add 2 tablespoons water.
Cooking time: 3–4 minutes
Serves 4

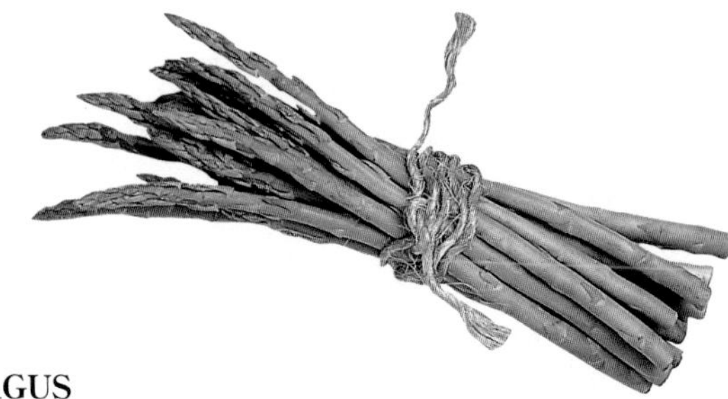

ASPARAGUS
Quantity: 250 g (8 oz)
Preparation: Trim any woody ends from the spears. Add 3 tablespoons water.
Cooking time: 2–3 minutes
Serves 4

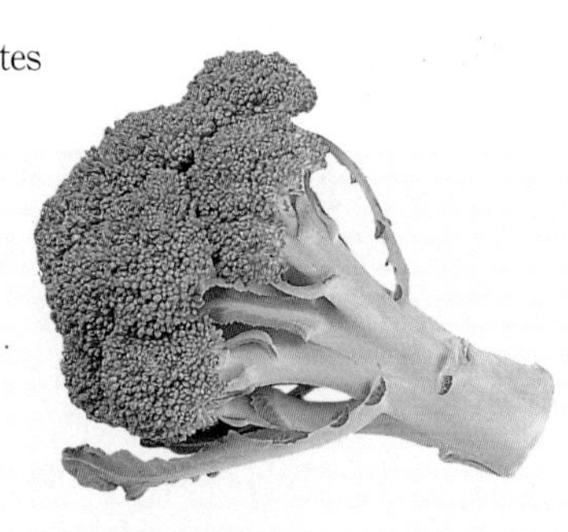

BROCCOLI
Quantity: 250 g (8 oz)
Preparation: Cut into florets and make a cut in the base of each stalk. Add 2 tablespoons water.
Cooking time: 3–4 minutes
Serves 4–6

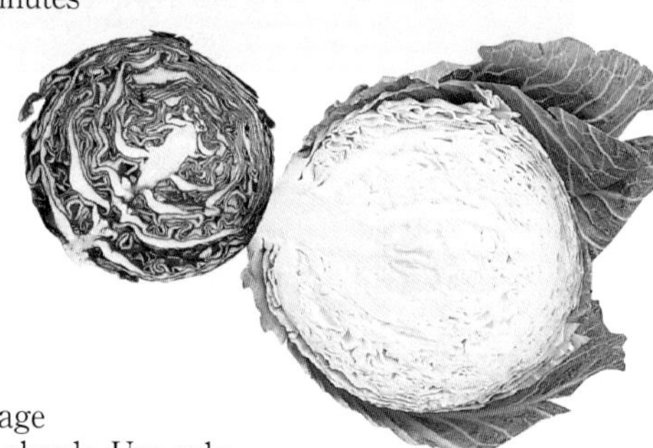

CABBAGE
Quantity: Half a cabbage
Preparation: Cut into shreds. Use only the water clinging to the cabbage after washing, add a small knob of butter if you like.
Cooking time: 6–8 minutes
Serves 6

CAULIFLOWER
Quantity: Half a cauliflower
Preparation: Cut into florets, and make a cut in the base of each stalk. Add 2 tablespoons water.
Cooking time: 7–8 minutes
Serves 4–6

from the Microwave

CORN
Quantity: 2 cobs
Preparation: Remove husks and silk, dot with butter and wrap in plastic microwave wrap.
Cooking time: 6–8 minutes
Serves 2

ONIONS
Quantity: 250 g (8 oz)
Preparation: Slice finely. Add 1 tablespoon butter.
Cooking time: 3–4 minutes
Serves 4–6

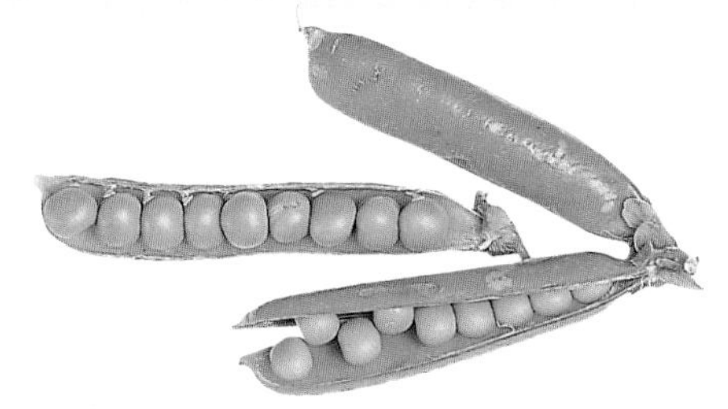

PEAS
Quantity: 250 g (8 oz)
Preparation: Remove peas from pods. Add 2 tablespoons water.
Cooking time: 3–5 minutes
Serves 4

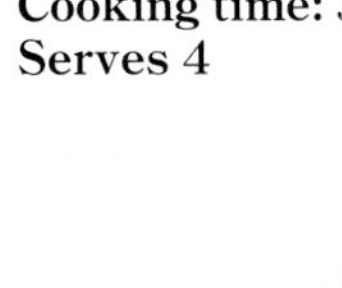

PUMPKIN
Quantity: 250 g (8 oz)
Preparation: Remove skin and seeds; cut into serving pieces. Add 2 tablespoons water.
Cooking time: 4–6 minutes
Serves 4

MUSHROOMS
Quantity: 250 g (8 oz)
Preparation: Wipe clean with paper towel and leave whole or slice if preferred. Dot with butter.
Cooking time: 3–5 minutes
Serves 4

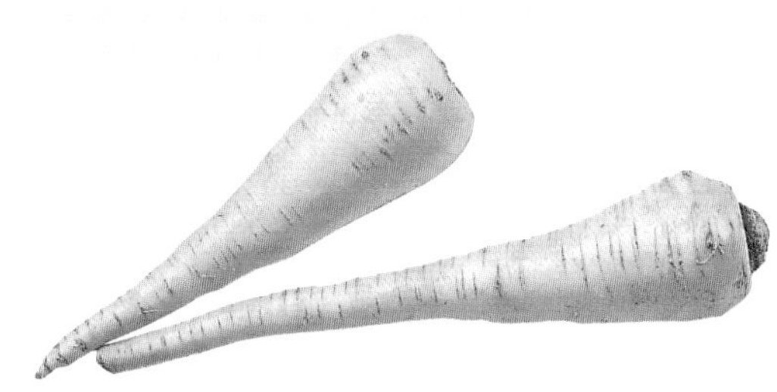

PARSNIPS
Quantity: 250 g (8 oz)
Preparation: Peel and slice. Add 2 tablespoons water.
Cooking time: 5–6 minutes
Serves 4

POTATOES
Quantity: 250 g (8 oz)
Preparation: Peel or scrub and cut into quarters. Add 2 tablespoons water.
Cooking time: 6–8 minutes
Serves 2

ZUCCHINI
Quantity: 250 g (8 oz)
Preparation: Trim ends and cut into thick slices. Dot with butter.
Cooking time: 3–4 minutes
Serves 4

ITALIAN MUSHROOMS

Preparation time: 20 minutes
Total cooking time: 17 minutes
Serves 4

30 g (1 oz) butter
1 onion, sliced
1 clove garlic, crushed
2 tomatoes, peeled and chopped
1 tablespoon tomato paste
3 tablespoons chicken stock
1 bay leaf
1/2 teaspoon black peppercorns
1 tablespoon thyme leaves
350 g (11 1/4 oz) button mushrooms

1 Melt the butter in a microwave-safe bowl on High (100%) for 30 seconds. Add the onion and garlic and cook on High (100%) for 3 minutes.
2 Add the tomatoes, tomato paste, chicken stock, bay leaf, peppercorns and thyme and stir to combine. Cook on High (100%) for 6 minutes, stirring after 2 and 4 minutes.
3 Stir in the mushrooms and cook for a further 7 minutes on High (100%), stirring halfway through cooking. Leave for 1–2 minutes before serving. Discard the bay leaf before serving. Delicious with crusty Italian bread.

COOK'S FILE

Note: To peel a tomato, score a cross in the base then place the tomato into a bowl of boiling water for 1 minute. Plunge into cold water and peel the skin away from the cross—it should come away easily.

Peel the tomatoes by plunging in boiling water, then chop the flesh.

Mix in the tomato, tomato paste, chicken stock, bay leaf, peppercorns and thyme.

The bay leaf adds flavour to the dish but should be removed before serving.

BEAN, ASPARAGUS AND PROSCIUTTO SALAD

Preparation time: 15 minutes
Total cooking time: 10 minutes
Serves 4

300 g (9 2/3 oz) green beans, topped and tailed
300 g (9 2/3 oz) asparagus, tough ends snapped off
100 g (3 1/3 oz) thinly sliced prosciutto
4 tablespoons extra virgin olive oil
2 tablespoons balsamic vinegar
shavings of Parmesan cheese, to serve

1 Wash the beans and asparagus, place in a microwave-safe dish and loosely cover. Cook on High (100%) for 7 minutes and then plunge into icy water. This will retain the green colour and make the vegetables crisp.
2 Place the slices of prosciutto in a single layer on a dish covered with paper towel (keeping it in a single layer prevents the prosciutto sticking together). Cover with another sheet of paper towel and cook on High (100%) for 3 minutes, or until the prosciutto is crisp (you may have to do this in two batches). Remove the prosciutto immediately from the paper before it cools and sticks.
3 Arrange the green beans and asparagus on a serving plate and drizzle with the olive oil and balsamic vinegar. Scatter over the pieces of crispy prosciutto and some Parmesan shavings, to serve.

COOK'S FILE

Hint: Use an ordinary potato peeler to make shavings from a wedge of Parmesan cheese.

Cover the beans and asparagus loosely and cook for 7 minutes.

Plunge the vegetables into icy water to stop the cooking process.

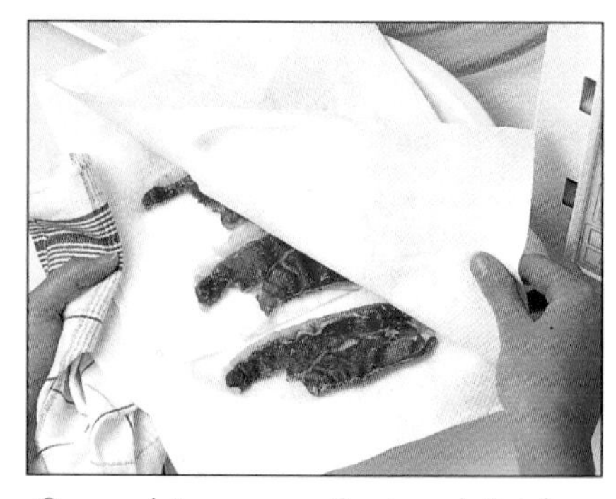

Once crisp, remove the prosciutto from the paper towels immediately.

Italian Mushrooms (top) with Bean, Asparagus and Prosciutto Salad

CORN AND BEAN SALAD

Preparation time: 10 minutes + overnight soaking
Total cooking time: 50 minutes
Serves 4

1/2 cup (105 g/3 1/2 oz) dried red kidney beans
1/2 cup (100 g/3 1/3 oz) haricot beans
30 g (1 oz) butter
1 onion, sliced
1 clove garlic, crushed
1 cup (150 g/4 3/4 oz) frozen corn kernels
2 tablespoons cream
2 tablespoons chopped fresh parsley

1 Soak the beans overnight, then drain and rinse. Place in a microwave-safe bowl and cover with boiling water. Cover and cook on High (100%) for 40 minutes; stir every 10 minutes. Leave for 5–10 minutes, then drain and set aside.

2 Melt the butter in a microwave-safe bowl on High (100%) for 30 seconds, add the onion and garlic and cook for 3 minutes. Stir in the beans and corn and cook for 3 minutes, until the corn is cooked; stir after 2 minutes.

3 Stir in the cream and parsley and season well with salt and pepper.

COOK'S FILE

Note: If you do not have time to soak the beans overnight, place them in a large bowl, cover well with boiling water, then cover tightly with plastic wrap and cook on High (100%) for 40 minutes, stirring every 10 minutes. Then continue with the recipe.

Put the beans in a bowl with water, cover and cook. Stir every 10 minutes.

Cook the onion and garlic in butter then stir in the beans and corn kernels.

Once all the vegetables are cooked, stir in the cream and parsley and season well.

BRAISED FENNEL

Preparation time: 20 minutes
Total cooking time: 23 minutes
Serves 6

3 medium fennel bulbs
30 g (1 oz) butter
2 onions, sliced
2 cloves garlic, crushed
425 g (13½ oz) can chopped tomatoes
½ cup (125 ml/4 fl oz) white wine
50 g (1⅔ oz) small Italian olives
1 tablespoon chopped thyme
½ teaspoon sugar
thyme sprigs, to garnish

1 Trim and discard the stalks from the fennel bulbs and cut lengthways into 1 cm (½ inch) slices; set aside. Place the butter in a large microwave-safe dish; melt on High (100%) for 30 seconds. Add the onion and garlic and cook for 3 minutes.

2 Add the tomatoes, wine, olives, thyme and sugar and mix well. Cook on High (100%) for 4 minutes, stirring after 2 minutes. Remove half the mixture from the dish.

3 Place the fennel slices in a single layer over the tomato mixture in the dish. Spoon the remaining tomato mixture over the fennel. Cover and cook on High (100%) for 15 minutes, turning and rearranging the fennel after 7 minutes and basting with the tomato mixture.

COOK'S FILE

Note: Braised fennel is delicious served as an accompaniment to roast lamb or beef.

Use a sharp knife to trim away the stalks from the fennel bulbs.

Add the tomatoes, wine, olives, thyme and sugar and mix well.

Arrange the fennel in a single layer and spoon the tomato mixture over the top.

FISH AND SHELLFISH

FISH ROLLS WITH LIME SAUCE

Preparation time: 30 minutes
Total cooking time: 14 minutes
Serves 4

4 white fish fillets (approximately 750 g/1½ lb)
500 g (1 lb) raw prawns
30 g (1 oz) butter
1 onion, finely chopped
2 cloves garlic, crushed
¼ cup (20 g/⅔ oz) fresh breadcrumbs
1 tablespoon chopped chives
lemon pepper

Lime Sauce
2 tablespoons lime juice
2 teaspoons grated lime rind
½ cup (125 ml/4 fl oz) cream
20 g (⅔ oz) butter, chopped

1 Remove any skin from the fish fillets and trim them into a neat shape. Remove any small bones with a pair of tweezers. Peel the prawns, remove the large back veins and chop the flesh roughly. Set aside.
2 Melt the butter in a microwave-safe bowl on High (100%) for 30 seconds. Add the onion and garlic and cook on High (100%) for 3 minutes. Stir in the prawns, breadcrumbs and chives and season well with lemon pepper.
3 Place the fish fillets on a board or work surface, skinned-side-up. Spoon a quarter of the prawn mixture into the centre of each fillet. Starting with the narrow end, fold up the two ends of the fish to enclose the filling and then secure with a couple of toothpicks. Place, seam-side-down, in a microwave-safe baking dish. Sprinkle with a little water, cover and cook on Medium High (75%) for 8 minutes. Leave for 2–3 minutes before serving with Lime Sauce.
4 To make Lime Sauce: Combine the lime juice, rind and cream in a microwave-safe bowl and heat on Medium (50%) for 2 minutes, stirring after 1 minute. Stir in the butter, piece by piece, mixing well after each addition. Spoon over the Fish Rolls.

COOK'S FILE

Note: Fish cooks particularly well in the microwave, as it stays very moist. For a lower fat version, serve the fish with a tomato sauce, rather than the Lime Sauce with cream.

Add the prawns, breadcrumbs, chives and lemon pepper to the onion and garlic.

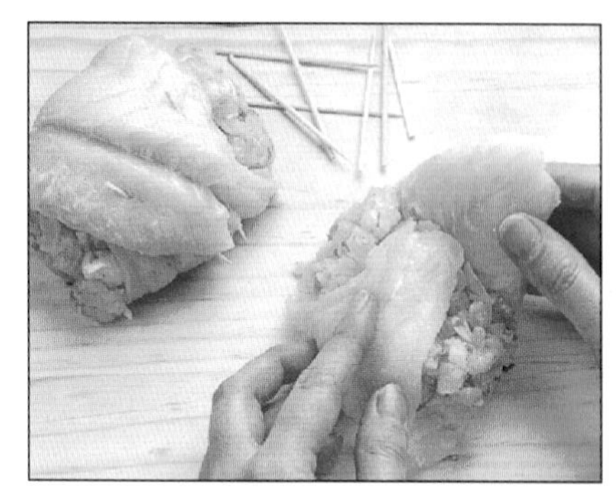

Fold up the ends of the fish over the filling and secure with toothpicks.

SALMON WITH HOLLANDAISE SAUCE

Preparation time: 10 minutes
Total cooking time: 10 minutes
Serves 4

4 pieces salmon fillet
200 g (6½ oz) butter
3 egg yolks
2 tablespoons lemon juice

1 Discard the skin from the salmon and remove any bones with a pair of tweezers. Place the salmon pieces in a microwave-safe dish; cover loosely. Cook for 3 minutes on High (100%) and then 4 minutes on Medium (50%). Remove from the microwave and keep warm while making the Hollandaise.

2 Melt the butter on High (100%) in a microwave-safe jug for 1 minute. Beat the egg yolks and lemon juice together in a microwave-safe bowl and add the melted butter, whisking well. Cook for 1 minute 20 seconds on Medium (50%), whisking every 20 seconds. The sauce should be well thickened and have the consistency of custard. Season to taste with salt and pepper.

3 Place the salmon on serving plates and spoon over the Hollandaise Sauce.

COOK'S FILE

Hint: Hollandaise is also delicious with steamed asparagus spears.

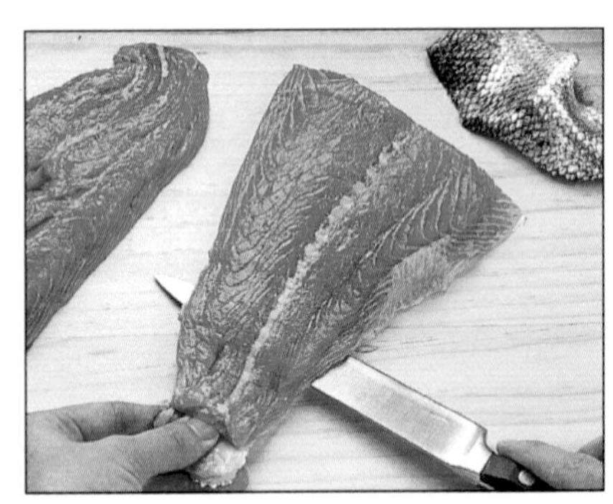

Cut the skin from the salmon. A little salt on your fingers helps you hold it firmly.

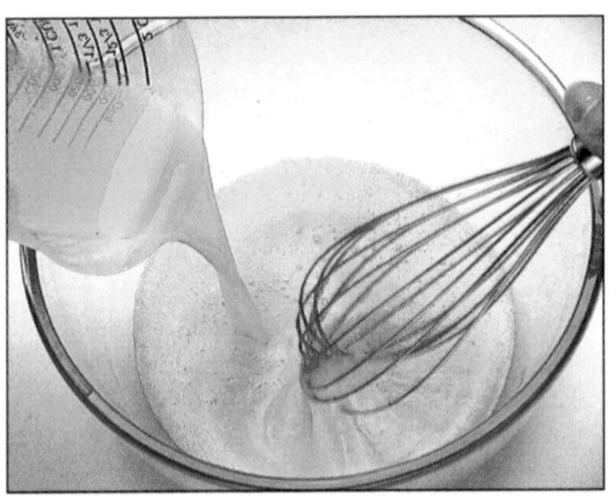

Whisk the melted butter into the beaten yolks and lemon juice.

Cook for 1 minute 20 seconds, whisking after every 20 seconds.

Stir the rice until it is well coated with the butter and onion mixture.

Stir in the stock and tomato paste. Cook for 8 minutes, then stir well.

Stir well and add the prawns, scallops, fish and octopus.

Leave the risotto for 5 minutes and then add the juice of two lemon wedges.

SEAFOOD RISOTTO

Preparation time: 25 minutes
Total cooking time: 25 minutes
Serves 4

50 g ($1^2/_3$ oz) butter
1 onion, chopped
200 g ($6^1/_2$ oz) arborio rice
3 cups (750 ml/24 fl oz) chicken or fish stock
2 teaspoons tomato paste
8 raw prawns, peeled and deveined, tails left intact
100 g ($3^1/_3$ oz) scallops
200 g ($6^1/_2$ oz) fish fillets, cut into bite-size pieces
4 baby octopus, cleaned, heads removed and cut in half
1 lemon, cut into wedges

1 Melt the butter in a microwave-safe casserole dish for 1 minute on High (100%). Stir in the onion and cook for 3 minutes on High (100%). Add the rice and stir until well coated with the butter and onion mixture. Cook on High (100%) for 2 minutes.
2 Stir in all the stock and the tomato paste and cook on High (100%) for 8 minutes. Stir well; cook for a further 8 minutes.
3 Stir well and then add the prawns, scallops, fish and octopus. Cook on High (100%) for 3 minutes, or until the seafood is cooked through.
4 Leave the risotto for 5 minutes to let the flavours develop. Season to taste with salt and freshly ground black pepper and squeeze in the juice from 2 of the lemon wedges. Serve with the remaining lemon wedges.

COOK'S FILE

Note: Arborio rice is best for risottos as it absorbs a lot of liquid, becoming creamy but maintaining a slight bite.

SCALLOPS AND PRAWNS IN COCONUT MILK

Preparation time: 25 minutes
Total cooking time: 7 minutes
Serves 4

500 g (1 lb) raw prawns, peeled and deveined, tails left intact
400 g (12 2/3 oz) scallops
3 tablespoons fresh lime juice
1 teaspoon chopped fresh ginger
1 tablespoon palm or soft brown sugar
1/2 teaspoon salt
200 ml (6 1/2 fl oz) coconut milk
1 tablespoon chopped fresh coriander
1 tablespoon chopped fresh mint
1/2 teaspoon chopped fresh red chilli

1 Mix together the prawns, scallops, lime juice, ginger, sugar, salt and coconut milk in a large microwave-safe bowl.
2 Cover loosely and cook on Medium High (75%) for 7 minutes, stirring after 5 minutes.
3 Leave for 5 minutes, then scatter with the coriander, mint and red chilli. Stir to combine. Serve with jasmine rice and a salad.

Mix together the prawns, scallops, sugar, lime juice, ginger, salt and coconut milk.

Cover loosely and stir after 5 minutes cooking time.

Leave to rest for 5 minutes, then scatter with coriander, mint and red chilli.

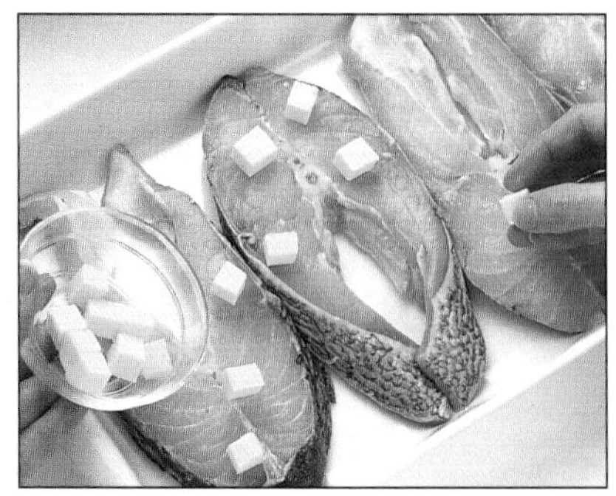

Arrange the fish in one layer and dot with the cubes of butter.

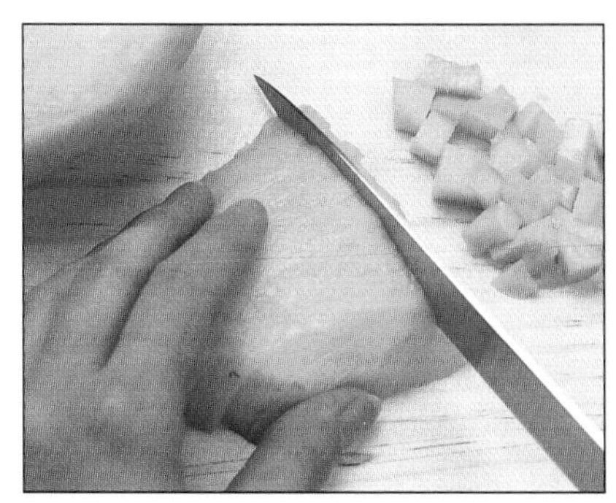

Peel the mango and dice the flesh into small cubes.

To prevent chilli burns, wear disposable gloves when handling chilli.

Stir the chopped coriander into the Mango Salsa, after warming.

FISH WITH WARM MANGO SALSA

Preparation time: 20 minutes
Total cooking time: 10 minutes
Serves 4

4 firm white fish steaks
30 g (1 oz) butter, cubed
1 mango
1/2 red onion, finely chopped
1/2 red capsicum, finely chopped
2 teaspoons lime juice
1 red chilli, seeded and finely chopped
1 tablespoon chopped coriander

1 Place the fish steaks in a large microwave-safe casserole dish and dot with the butter. Cover tightly and cook on Medium High (75%) for 6–8 minutes, or until cooked. Leave for 2–3 minutes.

2 Peel the mango and cut the flesh away from the seed. Chop the flesh into small pieces.

3 Put the mango in a microwave-safe bowl with the red onion, capsicum, lime juice and chilli; mix well. Heat in the microwave on Medium (50%) for 2 minutes, stirring after 1 minute. Stir through the coriander. Place the fish on a serving plate and spoon over the warm salsa.

COOK'S FILE

Variation: We used blue-eyed cod but Mango Salsa teams well with any white fish, such as swordfish.

FISH FILLETS WITH LEMON HERB BUTTER

Preparation time: 10 minutes
Total cooking time: 7 minutes
Serves 4

100 g (3 1/3 oz) butter
2 teaspoons finely grated lemon rind
3 tablespoons lemon juice
2 tablespoons finely chopped fresh herbs such as chives or parsley
4 white fish fillets (about 200 g/6 1/2 oz each)

1 Put the butter in a microwave-safe jug and cook on High (100%) for 2 minutes, until melted. Add the lemon rind and juice and the herbs.

2 Put the fish in a microwave-safe dish and cook, covered, on High (100%) for about 4 minutes, or until the fish flakes easily with a fork. Leave to stand for 2 minutes.

3 Reheat the Lemon Herb Butter for 30 seconds and pour over the fish. Garnish with whole chives.

COOK'S FILE

Variation: Use lime instead of lemon.

Melt the butter, then add the lemon rind, juice and herbs.

Test that the fish is cooked—it should flake easily.

Reheat the Lemon Herb Butter and pour over the fish fillets.

SALMON PATTIES WITH DILL SAUCE

Preparation time: 30 minutes
Total cooking time: 10 minutes
Serves 4

Salmon Patties
415 g (13 oz) can red salmon
1 onion, grated
1 cup (230 g/7 1/3 oz) mashed potatoes
1/2 cup (60 g/2 oz) grated Cheddar cheese
2 tablespoons chopped parsley
1 egg, lightly beaten
1 tablespoon lemon juice
freshly ground black pepper
20 g (2/3 oz) butter
1 cup (80 g/2 2/3 oz) fresh breadcrumbs

Dill Sauce
1 cup (250 ml/8 fl oz) crème fraîche
1 tablespoon lemon juice
2 tablespoons chopped dill
lemon pepper

1 To make Salmon Patties: Drain the salmon, removing any large bones and skin. Flake with a fork and then combine with the onion, potato, cheese, parsley, egg and lemon juice and season with black pepper to taste. Mix well with your hands. Divide into 8 portions and roll into patties.

2 Place the butter into a shallow microwave-safe dish and melt on High (100%) for 30 seconds. Stir in the breadcrumbs and cook on High (100%) for 5–6 minutes, or until the crumbs are golden brown, stirring frequently. Allow to cool.

3 Roll the patties in the breadcrumbs and place around the outer edge of a shallow microwave-safe dish or plate. Cook on High (100%) for 2 minutes. Carefully turn the patties with a spatula and cook the other side for a further 2 minutes on High (100%). Serve with Dill Sauce.

4 To make Dill Sauce: Put the crème fraîche, lemon juice, dill and lemon pepper to taste in a bowl and mix well.

Mix the salmon, onion, potato, cheese, parsley, egg, lemon juice and pepper.

Cook the breadcrumbs until golden brown and break up any lumps with a fork.

Roll each salmon patty in the cooled breadcrumbs.

Fish Fillets with Lemon Herb Butter (top) and Salmon Patties with Dill Sauce

TROUT WITH WILD RICE STUFFING

Preparation time: 15 minutes
Total cooking time: 12 minutes
Serves 2

30 g (1 oz) butter
100 g (3 1/3 oz) mushrooms, finely chopped
2 spring onions, chopped
1/2 cup (75 g/2 1/2 oz) cooked wild rice
1/2 cup (95 g/3 1/4 oz) cooked brown rice
2 teaspoons grated lemon rind
1 tablespoon lemon juice
1/2 teaspoon lemon pepper
2 rainbow trout
lemon or lime wedges, to serve

1 Melt the butter in a microwave-safe bowl on High (100%) for 30 seconds. Add the mushrooms and spring onions and cook on High (100%) for 1 minute 30 seconds.

2 Stir in the cooked rice, lemon rind, juice and lemon pepper. Season to taste with salt and pepper.

3 Wipe inside the fish with paper towels. Stuff the trout with the rice mixture and place, head to tail, in a microwave-safe dish with their backbones facing outwards. Spoon any remaining filling between the fish. Cover the dish loosely and cook on Medium High (75%) for 10 minutes.

4 Leave the fish covered for a couple of minutes and then check that they are fully cooked (the flesh should flake easily with a fork). Serve with lime or lemon wedges.

COOK'S FILE

Note: Pierce the eyes of the trout before microwaving, or ask your fishmonger to remove them. If the fish are very thick, make a few cuts to help even cooking. You might also like to trim away the fins.

Stir in the cooked rice, lemon juice and rind and the lemon pepper.

Stuff the trout with the rice filling and place in the microwave dish.

Place the fish, backbones facing outwards so the thinnest part is in the centre.

Remove the zest from the lemons, taking care to avoid any bitter pith.

Top the julienne vegetables with butter, thyme, wine, lemon juice and pepper.

Fold in the edges of the paper and scrunch up to make a parcel.

Check that the fish is cooked—it should flake easily with a fork.

FISH IN PARCHMENT

Preparation time: 20 minutes
Total cooking time: 8 minutes
Serves 4

4 fish fillets (about 200 g/6½ oz each), skinned and boned
½ leek, cut into julienne strips (see note)
1 carrot, cut into julienne strips
zest of 2 lemons
4 teaspoons butter
4 sprigs fresh lemon thyme
1 tablespoon white wine
1 tablespoon lemon juice

1 Place each fish fillet diagonally onto a separate piece of greaseproof paper, large enough to wrap the fillet completely.
2 Divide the julienne vegetables and lemon zest into four portions and sprinkle over the fish fillets. Top each with a teaspoon of butter, a sprig of thyme, 1 teaspoon wine, 1 teaspoon lemon juice and freshly ground black pepper to taste.
3 Fold in the edges of the paper and scrunch up to make a parcel which encloses the fish and filling.
4 Arrange the parcels lenthways around the microwave turntable and cook on High (100%) for 8 minutes. Open up one parcel to check that the fish is cooked (it should look opaque and flake easily with a fork). Serve the fish on individual plates, allowing everyone to open up their own parcel.

COOK'S FILE

Note: Julienne strips are uniform matchstick-sized strips of vegetables which cook quickly and evenly.

Savoury Sauces

TOMATO PASTA SAUCE

Cut small crosses in the bases of 6 tomatoes and place in a heatproof bowl. Cover with boiling water, leave for 1 minute, then plunge into cold water and peel the skin away from the cross. Roughly chop the tomato flesh and combine in a microwave-safe bowl with 2 crushed cloves of garlic, 2 teaspoons sugar and 1 tablespoon each of extra virgin olive oil and red wine vinegar. Cover loosely with plastic wrap and cook on High (100%) for 10 minutes, stirring after 5 minutes. Leave for 5 minutes before serving, over pasta, or with chicken or steak. Serves 4.

SATAY SAUCE

In a large microwave-safe bowl, combine 1/2 cup (125 g/4 oz) smooth peanut butter, 1 cup (250 ml/8 fl oz) chicken stock, 1 tablespoon lime juice, 1 teaspoon ground cumin, 1/2 teaspoon chilli flakes, 1 tablespoon soy sauce, 1 crushed clove garlic, 2 teaspoons finely grated ginger and 1 small grated onion. Cook on High (100%) for 6 minutes, stirring every 2 minutes. Serve with grilled or barbecued beef or chicken. Makes 1 1/2 cups (375 ml/12 fl oz).

PLUM SAUCE

Drain an 825 g (1 lb 11 oz) can of plums, reserving 3/4 cup (185 ml/6 fl oz) of the liquid. Remove the stones from the plums and roughly chop the flesh. In a microwave-safe bowl, combine 1 tablespoon oil, 1 finely chopped onion and 1 teaspoon freshly grated ginger. Cook on High (100%) for 2 minutes. Stir in the plums, reserved plum liquid and 1 tablespoon dry sherry. Cook on High (100%) for 4 minutes. Cool slightly, then process or blend until smooth. Serve with pork or chicken. Makes 1 cup (250 ml/8 fl oz).

APPLE SAUCE

Peel, core and chop 5 green apples and place in a microwave-safe bowl with 2 tablespoons water and 1 tablespoon lemon juice. Cook on High (100%) for 7 minutes. Add 1 tablespoon sugar, 1/4 teaspoon ground nutmeg and a pinch of ground cinnamon and mash through with a fork. For a smoother sauce, purée in a food processor. Makes 3 cups (750 ml/ 24 fl oz).

BARBECUE SAUCE

Combine 1 tablespoon oil, 1 finely chopped small onion and 1 crushed clove of garlic in a microwave-safe bowl. Cook on High (100%) for 2 minutes. Add 2 tablespoons soft brown sugar, 1/3 cup (80 ml/2 3/4 fl oz) tomato sauce and 1 tablespoon each of malt vinegar, Worcestershire sauce and tomato paste. Mix well and cook for 4 minutes on High (100%), stirring occasionally. Serve with grilled or barbecued meats. Makes 3/4 cup (185 ml/6 fl oz).

LEMON SAUCE

Combine 3 tablespoons lemon juice, 1/2 cup (125 ml/ 4 fl oz) water, 1 teaspoon finely grated lemon rind, 1 tablespoon sugar and 1 teaspoon grated ginger in a microwave-safe bowl and cook on High (100%) for 2 minutes. Mix together 2 teaspoons cornflour and 1 tablespoon water until smooth and then stir into the lemon mixture. Cook on High (100%) for 1 minute, stirring after 30 seconds, until the mixture boils and thickens slightly. Serve with fish or chicken. Makes 3/4 cup (185 ml/6 fl oz).

Clockwise from left: Tomato Pasta Sauce; Satay Sauce; Apple Sauce; Lemon Sauce; Barbecue Sauce; Plum Sauce

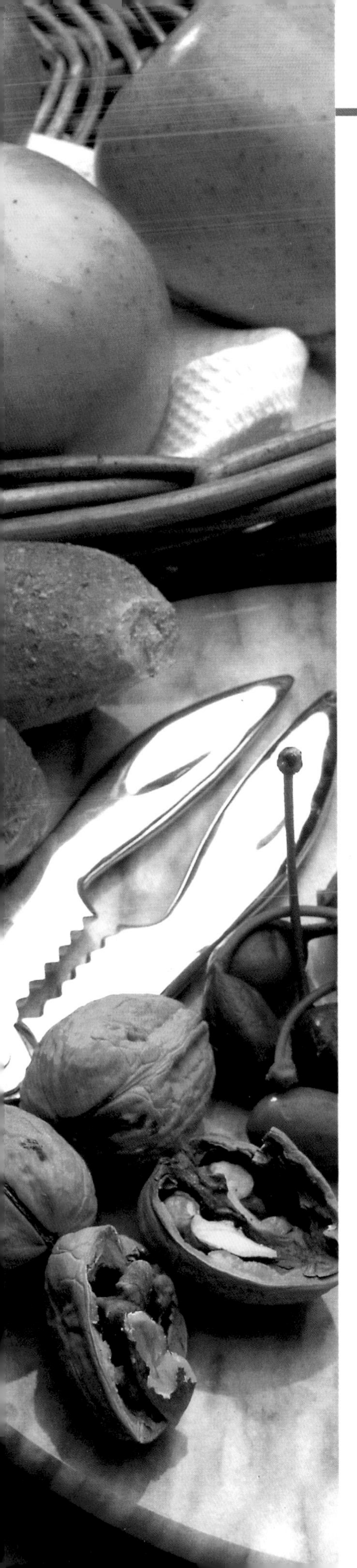

CHICKEN

PAPRIKA CHICKEN

Preparation time: 20 minutes
Total cooking time: 25 minutes
Serves 4

1 tablespoon oil
1 kg (2 lb) chicken breast fillets, cut into thin strips
30 g (1 oz) butter
1 onion, chopped
1 clove garlic, crushed
3 teaspoons Hungarian paprika
425 g (13 1/2 oz) can chopped tomatoes
1 tablespoon tomato paste
3 tablespoons chicken stock
3/4 cup (185 g/6 oz) sour cream

1 Heat the oil in a frying pan over moderate heat and fry the chicken strips, in several batches, until they are well browned.

2 Melt the butter in a microwave-safe bowl on High (100%) for 30 seconds, add the onion and garlic and cook for 3 minutes. Add the paprika, tomatoes, tomato paste and chicken stock and mix well. Cook on High (100%) for 3 minutes.

3 Stir in the browned chicken strips. Cover and then cook on High (100%) for 10 minutes; stir after 5 minutes.

4 Mix in the sour cream and season to taste. Cook on Medium (50%) for 3 minutes, stirring every minute. Leave for 10 minutes, then serve with rice, noodles or crusty bread.

COOK'S FILE

Note: Leaving for 10 minutes before serving lets the flavours develop and the meat tenderise. If possible, make the day before and reheat thoroughly on Medium (50%).

Variation: Use chicken thigh fillets instead of chicken breast fillets.

Brown the chicken in batches so that it fries rather than stews.

Add the paprika, tomatoes, tomato paste and chicken stock.

Add the browned chicken strips and stir well. Cook for 10 minutes.

Mix in the sour cream and season to taste with salt and pepper.

CAJUN CHICKEN CASSEROLE

Preparation time: 15 minutes
Total cooking time: 30 minutes
Serves 4

1 kg (2 lb) chicken pieces
1 tablespoon Cajun seasoning
1 tablespoon oil
30 g (1 oz) butter
2 tablespoons plain flour
1 onion, chopped
1 green capsicum, chopped
2 celery sticks, chopped
425 g (13½ oz) can chopped tomatoes
2 tablespoons tomato paste
1½ cups (375 ml/12 fl oz) chicken stock
1 bay leaf
½ teaspoon chilli powder
1 tablespoon chopped fresh thyme

1 Sprinkle the chicken pieces with Cajun seasoning. Heat the oil in a frying pan and brown the chicken pieces in batches until golden, turning frequently. Set aside.

2 In a microwave-safe casserole dish, melt the butter on High (100%) for 30 seconds. Stir in the flour and cook for 3 minutes, until golden, stirring twice during cooking. Stir in the onion, capsicum and celery and cook on High (100%) for 4 minutes.

3 Stir in the tomatoes, tomato paste, chicken stock, bay leaf, chilli and thyme. Add the browned chicken to the mixture, placing the thickest part of the chicken at the outer edges of the dish. Cook on Medium High (75%) for 16 minutes, stirring and rearranging the chicken after 6 and 12 minutes. Leave for 5 minutes before serving with crusty bread.

Brown the chicken in batches so it fries rather than stews. Turn frequently.

Melt the butter, stir in the flour and cook until golden.

Arrange the chicken with the thickest parts to the outside edge of the dish.

CHICKEN LIVERS WITH MUSHROOMS, ONIONS AND WILD RICE

Preparation time: 25 minutes
Total cooking time: 55 minutes
Serves 4

1 cup (210 g/6¾ oz) brown and wild rice blend
1½ cups (375 ml/12 fl oz) hot chicken stock
30 g (1 oz) butter
2 onions, finely sliced into rings
2 cloves garlic, crushed
5 whole chicken livers (about 500 g/1 lb)
250 g (8 oz) mushrooms, sliced
3 tablespoons chopped parsley

1 Place the rice in a deep microwave-safe casserole dish or bowl and pour over the chicken stock and 2½ cups (600 ml/20 fl oz) boiling water. Cover tightly with a lid or plastic wrap and cook on High (100%) for 45 minutes, stirring twice during cooking. Remove from the microwave and leave to stand for 5 minutes. Toss with a fork and set aside.
2 Place the butter into a large microwave-safe bowl and melt on High (100%) for 30 seconds. Add the onion rings and garlic and cook on High (100%) for 3 minutes.
3 Clean the chicken livers under running water, removing any sinew and membrane, then cut into quarters. Add to the onion mixture with the mushrooms. Cover and cook on High (100%) for 4 minutes, stirring after 2 minutes. Season well.
4 Fold the cooked rice through the chicken liver mixture. Reheat on High (100%) for 3 minutes, stirring after 2 minutes. Stir through the chopped parsley and serve.

Put the rice in a bowl with the chicken stock and water and cover tightly.

Leave the rice to stand for 5 minutes, then toss with a fork and set aside.

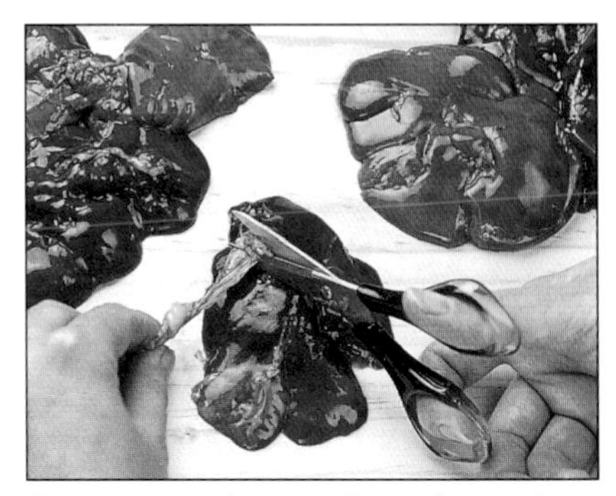

Remove any sinew and membrane from the chicken livers with a pair of scissors.

Fold the cooked rice through the chicken liver mixture.

COOK'S FILE

Note: Wild rice is comparatively expensive and is sold as a blend with brown rice to make it better value.

APRICOT CHICKEN

Preparation time: 10 minutes
Total cooking time: 17 minutes
Serves 4

4 chicken breast fillets
1 tablespoon oil
100 g (3 1/3 oz) dried apricots
1 cup (250 ml/8 fl oz) apricot nectar
1/2 cup (125 ml/4 fl oz) chicken stock
30 g (1 oz) French onion soup mix
chopped parsley, to garnish

1 Trim away any excess fat from the chicken, then cut into large chunks. Heat the oil in a frying pan and brown the pieces well in two batches.

2 Place the chicken pieces, apricots, apricot nectar, chicken stock and French onion soup mix into a large microwave-safe casserole dish. Mix well and cook on Medium High (75%) for 12 minutes; stir after 6 minutes.

3 Season with salt and pepper and leave for 10 minutes before serving. Sprinkle with parsley to serve.

COOK'S FILE

Note: If possible, make a day in advance, keep refrigerated and reheat thoroughly on Medium (50%).

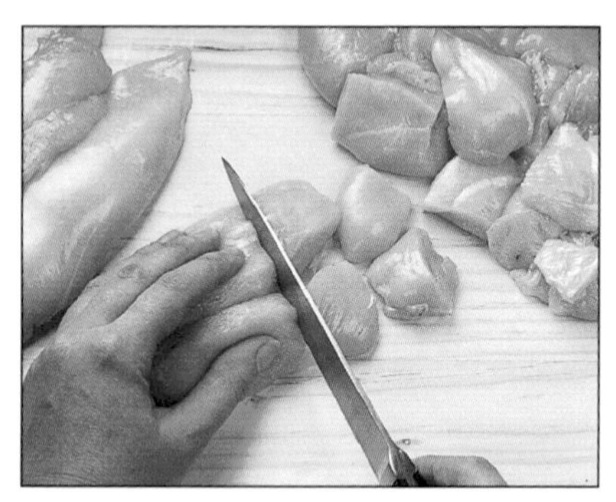

Trim away any excess fat, then cut the chicken into large chunks.

Combine the chicken, apricots, apricot nectar, stock and soup mix.

Season stews and casseroles after microwaving—salt can toughen the meat.

CHICKEN AND CHORIZO CASSEROLE

Preparation time: 20 minutes
Total cooking time: 18 minutes
Serves 4

8 chicken thigh fillets, chopped
1 tablespoon oil
1 onion, finely chopped
2 cloves garlic, crushed
2 tablespoons tomato paste
1 red capsicum, seeded and chopped
1 teaspoon hot paprika
1 bay leaf
1/2 cup (125 ml/4 fl oz) chicken stock
1/2 cup (125 ml/4 fl oz) red wine
1 tablespoon sugar
180 g (5 3/4 oz) chorizo sausage, thinly sliced
12 black olives

1 Cut away any excess fat and sinew from the chicken thigh fillets and then chop into large chunks. Place the oil, onion and garlic in a microwave-safe casserole dish and cook on High (100%) for 3 minutes. Stir in the chicken, tomato paste, red capsicum, paprika, bay leaf, chicken stock, red wine and sugar.

2 Cover and cook on High (100%) for 10 minutes, stirring the chicken pieces around in the casserole every couple of minutes to ensure that they cook evenly. Add the chorizo sausage and cook on High (100%) for 5 minutes.

3 Stir in the black olives and season to taste with salt and black pepper. Leave for 10 minutes to allow the flavours to develop, then serve with warm crusty Italian bread.

COOK'S FILE

Note: If possible, make a day ahead to let the flavours develop. Keep refrigerated and reheat thoroughly on Medium (50%).

Add the chicken, tomato paste, capsicum, paprika, bay leaf, stock, wine and sugar.

Cook for 10 minutes; add the chorizo sausage and cook for 5 minutes more.

Stir in the black olives and seasoning, then leave for the flavours to develop.

CHICKEN PILAF

Preparation time: 15 minutes
Total cooking time: 20 minutes
Serves 4

1 small barbecued chicken
50 g (1 2/3 oz) butter
1 onion, finely chopped
2 cloves garlic, crushed
300 g (9 2/3 oz) basmati rice
1 tablespoon currants
2 tablespoons finely chopped dried apricots
1 teaspoon ground cinnamon
pinch of ground cardamom
3 cups (750 ml/24 fl oz) chicken stock
1/4 cup (7 g/1/4 oz) fresh coriander, chopped

1 Remove the skin and excess fat from the chicken and chop the meat into even, bite-sized pieces.
2 Melt the butter in a microwave-safe bowl on High (100%) for 30 seconds. Stir in the onion and garlic and cook on High (100%) for 2 minutes. Add the rice, currants, apricots and spices and stir until well coated.
3 Pour in the stock and stir well. Cover and cook on High (100%) for 14 minutes; stir after 8 minutes. Leave for 5 minutes without uncovering.
4 Add the chicken and reheat on High (100%) for 4 minutes, stirring after 2 minutes. Stir through the coriander to serve.

Add the rice, currants, apricots, spices and stir to coat with butter.

Pour in the stock, then cover and cook, stirring after 8 minutes.

Add the chicken and reheat. Stir through the chopped coriander before serving.

Add the garlic, tomatoes, tomato paste, wine, sugar, oregano and bay leaf.

Arrange the chicken in the dish and spoon over the tomato mixture.

Rearrange the chicken pieces so that they all cook evenly.

Before serving, remove the bay leaf and add the black olives.

CHICKEN CACCIATORE

Preparation time: 15 minutes
Total cooking time: 27 minutes
Serves 4

1 tablespoon olive oil
1 onion, thickly sliced
2 cloves garlic, crushed
425 g (13½ oz) can tomatoes, roughly chopped
2 tablespoons tomato paste
¼ cup (60 ml/2 fl oz) white wine
1 teaspoon sugar
1 teaspoon oregano
1 bay leaf
1 kg (2 lb) chicken thigh cutlets
12 black olives

1 Place the oil and onion into a large microwave-safe casserole dish and cook on High (100%) for 2 minutes. Add the garlic, tomatoes and their juice, tomato paste, wine, sugar, oregano and bay leaf. Stir well.

2 Remove any excess fat from the chicken and arrange a single layer in the casserole dish. Spoon the tomato mixture over the chicken. Cover the dish loosely and cook on High (100%) for 15 minutes.

3 Remove the casserole dish from the microwave; stir and rearrange the chicken pieces to ensure that they cook evenly. Return to the microwave and cook for another 10 minutes on Medium (50%).

4 Leave the casserole for 10 minutes before serving to allow the flavours to develop and the chicken to tenderise. Just before serving, remove the bay leaf and stir in the black olives. Serve with pasta or rice.

THAI CHICKEN CURRY

Preparation time: 30 minutes
Total cooking time: 18 minutes
Serves 4

1 tablespoon oil
1 onion, chopped
1–2 tablespoons Thai green curry paste
1/2 cup (125 ml/4 fl oz) chicken stock
500 g (1 lb) chicken fillets, cut into chunks
100 g (3 1/3 oz) green beans or snake beans, cut into short lengths
1/2 red capsicum, chopped
1/2 cup (125 ml/4 fl oz) coconut milk
1 tablespoon fish sauce
1 tablespoon lime juice
1 teaspoon grated lime rind
2 teaspoons palm or soft brown sugar
1/4 cup (15 g/1/2 oz) chopped coriander

1 Heat the oil in a microwave-safe casserole dish on High (100%) for 2 minutes. Add the onion and curry paste and cook on High (100%) for 1 minute.

2 Stir in the stock, chicken, green or snake beans and capsicum. Cook for 10 minutes on Medium (50%), stirring well after 5 minutes.

3 Stir the coconut milk, fish sauce, lime juice, rind and sugar into the chicken mixture. Cook on Medium (50%) for 5 minutes, stirring after 3 minutes. Leave for 2–3 minutes before serving. Stir through the chopped coriander and serve with steamed jasmine rice.

Heat the oil and then add the onion and curry paste.

Cook for 10 minutes, stirring well after 5 minutes to ensure even cooking.

Stir in the coconut milk, fish sauce, lime juice, rind and sugar.

LEMON AND OLIVE CHICKEN

Preparation time: 20 minutes
Total cooking time: 12 minutes
Serves 4

155 g (5 oz) green olives, pitted
155 g (5 oz) black olives, pitted
60 g (2 oz) sun-dried tomatoes
2 teaspoons grated lemon rind
2 tablespoons lemon juice
1/4 cup (15 g/1/2 oz) finely chopped parsley
4 chicken breast fillets

1 Process the pitted olives, sun-dried tomatoes, lemon zest, lemon juice and parsley in a blender or food processor to make a purée.

2 Score three diagonal slashes into each chicken fillet. Place the chicken in a microwave-safe casserole dish, spoon over the olive purée and spread all over the fillets.

3 Cover the dish and cook on Medium High (75%) for 10 minutes, then leave to stand for 10 minutes before serving to allow the flavours to develop and the chicken to tenderise. If necessary, reheat thoroughly on High (100%).

Process the olives, tomatoes, parsley, lemon rind and juice into a purée.

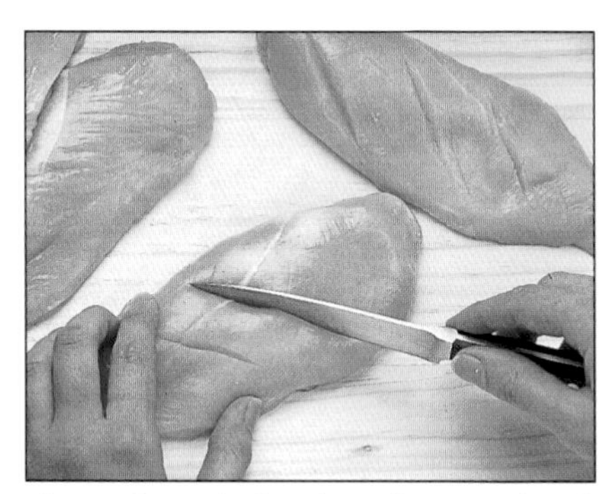

Score three slashes into the top of each fillet to hold the purée.

Spread the purée evenly over the fillets with the back of a spoon.

DELICIOUS MEAT DISHES

BEEF CURRY

Preparation time: 20 minutes
Total cooking time: 1 hour
Serves 4

2 tablespoons vegetable oil
750 g (1 1/2 lb) rump steak, cut into cubes
1 large onion, sliced into rings
1 clove garlic, crushed
2 teaspoons grated fresh ginger
1 teaspoon chilli powder
1 teaspoon garam masala
1 teaspoon turmeric
1 teaspoon cumin seeds
1/2 teaspoon fennel seeds
1 cup (250 ml/8 fl oz) beef stock
1/2 cup (125 ml/4 fl oz) coconut milk

1 Heat 1 tablespoon of the oil in a frying pan. Brown the steak in batches over high heat, not turning until each side is deep brown.

2 Place the other tablespoon of oil in a microwave-safe casserole dish and stir in the onion and garlic. Cook on High (100%) for 3 minutes. Add the ginger, chilli powder, garam masala, turmeric, cumin and fennel seeds and cook for 2 minutes on High (100%).

3 Stir in the browned beef and beef stock. Cover and cook on Medium Low (40%) for 40 minutes. Add the coconut milk and cook, uncovered, on Medium Low (40%) for 4 minutes.

4 Leave for at least 10 minutes before serving as this allows the flavours to develop and the meat to tenderise. If necessary, reheat on Medium Low (40%) for 4 minutes, stirring after 2 minutes. Season to taste and serve with basmati rice and chutney.

COOK'S FILE

Note: As with all casseroles and stews (whether they are made in the microwave or conventional oven), you will get the best flavour if you make the dish a day ahead, store in the refrigerator and reheat gently.

Brown the meat in small batches so that it fries rather than stews in its juice.

Add the ginger, chilli powder, garam masala, turmeric, cumin and fennel seeds.

BEEF-STUFFED CAPSICUMS

Preparation time: 30 minutes
Total cooking time: 45 minutes
Serves 4

4 medium capsicums
2 tablespoons olive oil
1 onion, chopped
1 clove garlic, crushed
500 g (1 lb) beef mince
1 celery stick, finely chopped
100 g (3 1/3 oz) long-grain white rice
2 tomatoes, finely chopped
1 tablespoon tomato paste
1/2 cup (125 ml/4 fl oz) chicken stock
2 teaspoons thyme leaves
1 teaspoon chopped fresh basil
1 zucchini, finely chopped
1 cup (125 g/4 oz) grated Cheddar or Parmesan cheese

1 Cut each capsicum in half crossways and remove the seeds and membrane. Trim the bases so the capsicums sit flat. Place the oil in a frying pan, add the onion and garlic and cook for 1 minute. Add the mince and brown for 5 minutes, stirring well to break up any lumps.

2 Place the celery, rice, tomatoes, tomato paste, stock, thyme, basil and zucchini in a microwave-safe bowl. Add the mince mixture, cover loosely and cook on Medium High (75%) for 20 minutes; stir well after 10 minutes. Taste to check that the rice is fully cooked, if not, cook a further minute at a time until cooked. Season to taste with salt and black pepper.

3 Spoon the filling mixture evenly into the capsicums. Place in a large microwave-safe casserole dish. (Try to arrange the capsicums around the outside edge of the dish, as this will ensure more even cooking.) Cover loosely with cling wrap. Cook for 14 minutes on High (100%), then remove from the microwave.

4 Place the capsicums on a baking tray lined with foil and sprinkle with grated Cheddar or Parmesan cheese. Place under a hot grill until the cheese begins to bubble and turns golden brown. Serve with a green salad and crusty bread.

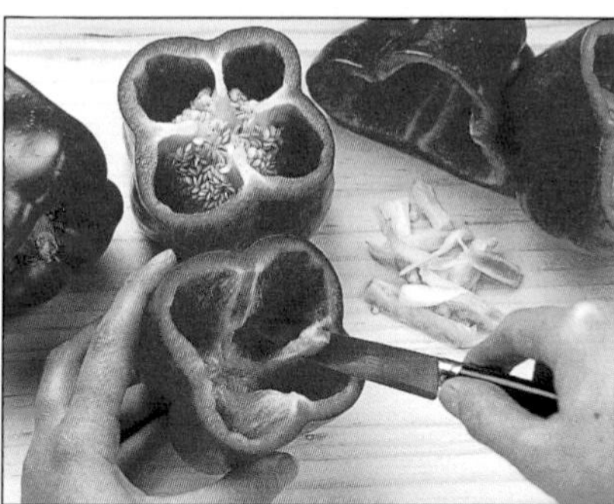

Cut each capsicum in half and remove the seeds and inner membrane.

Stir in the mince mixture and then cover loosely and cook for 20 minutes.

Spoon the filling mixture evenly into the capsicums and then cook for 14 minutes.

Top the capsicums with grated cheese and finish off under a hot grill.

BEEF STROGANOFF

Preparation time: 25 minutes
Total cooking time: 35 minutes
Serves 4

2 tablespoons vegetable oil
750 g (1 1/2 lb) steak, cut into thin strips
1 onion, sliced
1 clove garlic, crushed
3/4 cup (185 ml/6 fl oz) beef stock
1 tablespoon tomato paste
2 teaspoons Worcestershire sauce
100 g (3 1/3 oz) button mushrooms, sliced
3/4 cup (185 g/6 oz) sour cream
chopped parsley, to garnish

1 Heat half the oil in a frying pan and brown the steak well, in batches.
2 Place the remaining tablespoon of oil in a microwave-safe bowl, mix in the onion and garlic and cook on High (100%) for 3 minutes.
3 Add the browned beef to the bowl with the beef stock, tomato paste and Worcestershire sauce. Mix well, cover and cook on Medium Low (40%) for 25 minutes, stirring after 12 minutes.
4 Stir in the mushrooms and sour cream. Cook, uncovered, for 5 minutes on Medium Low (40%), stirring after 2 and 4 minutes. Season well with salt and pepper. Garnish with chopped parsley and serve with rice.

COOK'S FILE

Note: It is best to use sirloin steak.

Heat the oil in a frying pan and brown the beef strips well.

Add the browned beef, beef stock, tomato paste and Worcestershire sauce.

Stir in the mushrooms and sour cream and cook for a further 5 minutes.

SPAGHETTI WITH MEATBALLS

Preparation time: 30 minutes
Total cooking time: 30 minutes
Serves 4

500 g (1 lb) spaghetti

Meatballs
500 g (1 lb) beef mince
1 onion, finely chopped
1 clove garlic, crushed
3 tablespoons fresh breadcrumbs
1/2 teaspoon dried mixed herbs
1 egg, lightly beaten
2 tablespoons vegetable oil

Tomato Sauce
1 tablespoon oil
1 onion, finely chopped
1 clove garlic, crushed
425 g (13 1/2 oz) can crushed tomatoes
2 tablespoons tomato paste
1/2 cup (125 ml/4 fl oz) beef stock
1 teaspoon sugar
1 teaspoon dried oregano leaves
1/2 cup (60 g/2 oz) grated Cheddar cheese
2 tablespoons chopped parsley

1 Put the spaghetti in a large deep-sided microwave-safe dish, cover with boiling water and cook on High (100%) for 10 minutes, or until just tender. Drain and keep warm.

2 To make Meatballs: Place the mince, onion, garlic, breadcrumbs, mixed herbs and egg in a bowl and mix well with your hands. Roll 2 teaspoons of the mixture into a ball; repeat with the remainder. Heat the oil in a frying pan and brown the Meatballs in two batches.

3 To make Tomato Sauce: Place the oil, onion and garlic in a microwave-safe casserole dish and cook on High (100%) for 2 minutes. Mix in the tomatoes, tomato paste, beef stock, sugar and oregano and cook on High (100%) for 5 minutes.

4 Place the Meatballs in the Tomato Sauce and cook on Medium High (75%) for 5 minutes, stirring after 2 minutes. Serve over the spaghetti sprinkled with cheese and parsley.

Cook the spaghetti in plenty of water so it doesn't stick together.

Roll two teaspoons of the mixture at a time into balls.

Mix in the tomatoes, tomato paste, beef stock, sugar and oregano.

Place the browned meatballs in the Tomato Sauce and cook for 5 minutes.

CHILLI CON CARNE

Preparation time: 20 minutes
Total cooking time: 15 minutes
Serves 4–6

1 onion, peeled and chopped
2 cloves garlic, crushed
1–2 teaspoons finely chopped fresh red chilli
425 g (13½ oz) can crushed tomatoes
1 teaspoon ground cumin
1 teaspoon ground coriander
1 teaspoon ground cinnamon
500 g (1 lb) lean beef mince or chopped chuck steak
2 tablespoons red wine vinegar
15 g (½ oz) dark chocolate, chopped (or 1 tablespoon soft brown sugar)
425 g (13½ oz) canned red kidney beans, rinsed and drained
sour cream and grated Cheddar cheese, for serving

1 Place the onion, garlic, chilli and tomatoes in a microwave-safe casserole dish and stir in the cumin, coriander and cinnamon.

2 Cook, covered, on High (100%) for 7 minutes, stirring after 4 minutes. Stir again and add the beef, mixing it in thoroughly. Cook on High (100%) for 5 minutes; stir with a fork after 3 minutes to break up any lumps.

3 Add the vinegar, chocolate (or sugar) and kidney beans and cook on High (100%) for 3 minutes. Season to taste with salt and black pepper. Top with sour cream and cheese to serve.

COOK'S FILE

Note: The chocolate is traditionally used in Mexico. It adds a lovely flavour and is well worth trying.

Stir in the ground cumin, coriander and cinnamon.

Cook for 5 minutes. Stir after 3 minutes to break up any lumps.

Add the vinegar, chocolate, kidney beans and salt and pepper to taste.

BRAISED LAMB WITH BEANS

Preparation time: 20 minutes
Total cooking time: 30 minutes
Serves 4

1 tablespoon plain flour
12 lamb cutlets, trimmed
2 tablespoons olive oil
1 onion, finely chopped
2 cloves garlic, crushed
310 g (9¾ oz) can cannellini beans
100 ml (3¼ fl oz) white wine
100 ml (3¼ fl oz) chicken stock
1 teaspoon fresh rosemary leaves
2 teaspoons finely grated lemon rind
1 tablespoon lemon juice

1 Put the flour in a plastic bag, add the cutlets and toss well to coat. Shake off any excess flour. Place 1 tablespoon oil in a frying pan and brown the lamb well, in two batches, on both sides over high heat. Cook 1 minute further, then remove from the heat.

2 In a microwave-safe casserole dish, place the remaining tablespoon of oil with the onion and garlic. Cook on High (100%) for 3 minutes. Add the cannellini beans, wine, stock, rosemary, lemon rind and juice and cook on High (100%) for 5 minutes.

3 Place the cutlets into the bean mixture, stir to combine, then cover and cook for 7 minutes on Medium High (75%). Rearrange the cutlets to ensure even cooking and cook for another 7 minutes on Medium (50%).

4 Cover with foil and leave for at least 15 minutes before serving to allow the flavours to develop and the lamb to tenderise. Season with salt and black pepper, to taste, and serve.

Brown the lamb cutlets in two batches to give them room to fry, not stew.

Add the cannellini beans, wine, stock, rosemary, lemon rind and juice.

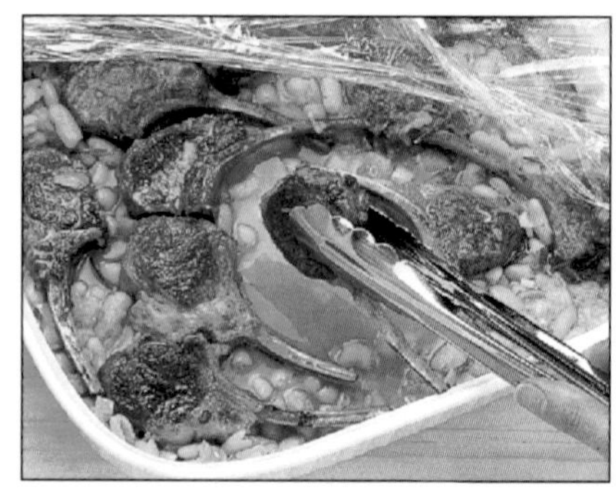

Rearrange the cutlets after 7 minutes to ensure even cooking.

Heat the oil and stir in the bacon, onions and garlic.

Add the beef and stir in the wine, beef stock and tomato paste.

Mix the flour with a little water to make a smooth paste to thicken the casserole.

Add the mushrooms at the end of the cooking time so they are not too soft.

BEEF IN RED WINE

Preparation time: 25 minutes
Total cooking time: 40 minutes
Serves 4

2 tablespoons olive oil
500 g (1 lb) rump steak, cut into thin strips
3 rashers bacon, chopped
8 baby onions
1 clove garlic, crushed
1/2 cup (125 ml/4 fl oz) red wine
3/4 cup (185 ml/6 fl oz) beef stock
2 tablespoons tomato paste
2 teaspoons plain flour
150 g (4 3/4 oz) button mushrooms, halved
2 tablespoons chopped parsley

1 Heat 1 tablespoon of the oil in a frying pan and cook the beef strips in batches until well browned. Place the second tablespoon oil in a microwave-safe casserole dish and stir in the bacon, onions and garlic. Cover with paper towel and cook on High (100%) for 4 minutes; stir after 2 minutes.

2 Add the browned beef strips to the bacon and onion mixture. Stir in the wine, beef stock and tomato paste. Cook, covered, on Medium Low (40%) for 25 minutes, stirring well after 12 minutes.

3 Mix the flour with a little water to form a paste and then stir into the casserole with the mushrooms. Cook on Medium (50%) for 5 minutes; stir after 3 minutes. Stir in the parsley and leave for 10 minutes before serving to let the flavours develop.

COOK'S FILE

Note: Don't compromise on quality—use as good a wine for cooking as you would for drinking.

IRISH STEW

Preparation time: 20 minutes
Total cooking time: 35 minutes
Serves 4

1 tablespoon vegetable oil
800 g (1 lb 10 oz) lamb chump chops, trimmed of fat
1 tablespoon plain flour
200 g (6½ oz) pickling onions, peeled
300 g (9⅔ oz) potatoes, peeled and cut into thick slices
250 g (8 oz) turnips, peeled and cut into thick slices
1½ cups (375 ml/12 fl oz) chicken stock
2 teaspoons dried oregano leaves

1 Heat the oil in a frying pan and brown the lamb chops in batches over high heat, not turning until each side is well browned.

2 Place the lamb in a microwave-safe casserole dish and sprinkle with flour.

3 Add the onions, potato and turnip and pour over the stock. Season to taste with black pepper and sprinkle with oregano. Cover and cook on Medium High (75%) for 30 minutes, stirring after every 10 minutes. Season with salt to taste. Leave for at least 10 minutes before serving: this allows the flavours to develop and the meat to tenderise. If possible, make a day in advance and reheat gently to serve.

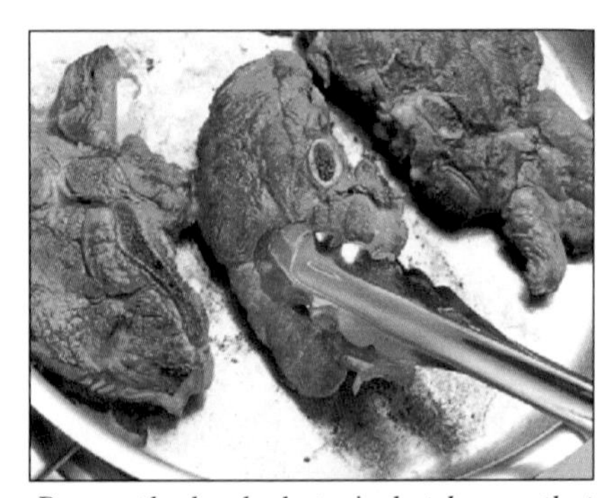

Brown the lamb chops in batches so that they fry rather than stew.

Put the chops in a casserole dish and sprinkle with flour.

Add the pickling onions, potato and turnip and pour over the stock.

Melt the butter in the microwave, then add the onion and garlic.

Spoon the veal and any cooking juices into the casserole dish.

Add the undrained tomato, caraway seeds, paprika, lemon rind and capsicum.

Season casseroles after cooking—liquid reduces and tastes become concentrated.

VEAL GOULASH

Preparation time: 20 minutes
Total cooking time: 25 minutes
Serves 4

800 g (1 lb 10 oz) veal
25 g (3/4 oz) butter
1 large onion, chopped
1 clove garlic, crushed
1 tablespoon olive oil
425 g (13 1/2 oz) can crushed tomatoes
1/2 teaspoon caraway seeds
1 tablespoon sweet paprika
1 teaspoon grated lemon rind
1 green capsicum, thinly sliced
sour cream, to serve

1 Trim away any fat from the veal and cut the meat into cubes. Melt the butter in a large microwave-safe casserole dish on High (100%) for 30 seconds. Add the onion and garlic; cook on High (100%) for 3 minutes.
2 Heat the oil in a frying pan and add the veal in batches, browning very well on all sides. Remove the pan from the heat and spoon the veal and cooking juices into the casserole dish.
3 Add the crushed tomato, caraway seeds, paprika, lemon rind and sliced capsicum and cover loosely. Cook for 15 minutes on Medium High (75%), stirrring after 8 minutes.
4 Leave the casserole to stand for at least 10 minutes before serving, longer if possible to allow the flavours to develop and the meat to tenderise in the sauce. Season to taste with salt and pepper and serve with sour cream and rice or pasta.

AMERICAN-STYLE RIBS

Preparation time: 15 minutes + overnight marinating
Total cooking time: 20 minutes
Serves 4–6

1 kg (2 lb) American-style pork ribs
2 cups (500 ml/16 fl oz) tomato sauce
1/4 cup (60 ml/2 fl oz) dry sherry
1/4 cup (60 ml/2 fl oz) Worcestershire sauce
3 cloves garlic, crushed
1/4 cup (45 g /1 1/2 oz) soft brown sugar
Tabasco sauce

1 Cut the racks of ribs into pieces with two or three ribs in each piece. Combine the tomato sauce, sherry, Worcestershire sauce, garlic and sugar in a large microwave-safe casserole dish; cook on High (100%) for 5 minutes. Add Tabasco to taste.
2 Arrange the ribs in the sauce in a single layer. Turn the ribs to coat well with the sauce, cover and cook on High (100%) for 7 minutes, turning occasionally to ensure even cooking.
3 Allow the ribs to cool. Refrigerate overnight or for at least several hours. Remove from the fridge 30 minutes before barbecuing. Place the ribs on a preheated barbecue grill and cook for 5–10 minutes, turning and brushing occasionally with the remaining sauce.

Cut the rack of ribs into even pieces, with two or three ribs in each piece.

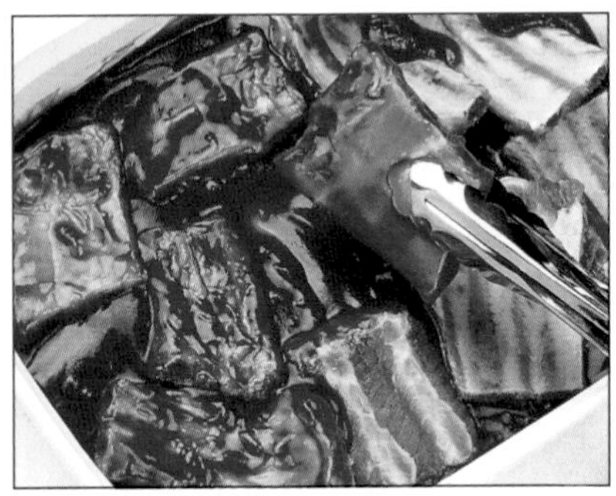

Turn the ribs over in the sauce so that they are completely coated.

Cook the ribs on a barbecue grill, turning and basting with the marinade.

PORK WITH APRICOTS AND PRUNES

Preparation time: 15 minutes
Total cooking time: 15 minutes
Serves 4

750 g (1½ lb) pork fillet
30 g (1 oz) butter
1 onion, thinly sliced
1 tablespoon plain flour
12 prunes, pitted
12 dried apricots
1 tablespoon apricot jam
½ cup (125 ml/4 fl oz) chicken stock
½ cup (125 ml/4 fl oz) white wine
2 bay leaves

1 Remove any sinew from the fillets and cut the pork into 2 cm (¾ inch) slices, cutting on the diagonal.
2 Melt the butter in a microwave-safe casserole dish for 30 seconds on High (100%). Add the onion; cook on High (100%) for 2 minutes. Stir in the flour; cook on High (100%) for 30 seconds.
3 Add the pork, prunes, apricots and jam. Pour in the stock and wine and stir until well combined. Add the bay leaves. Cover loosely and cook on High (100%) for 11 minutes, stirring every 4 minutes.
4 Cover with foil and leave the dish for 10 minutes to allow the flavours to develop and meat to tenderise. Season with salt and pepper and, if necessary, reheat on High (100%). Remove the bay leaves before serving.

Remove the sinew from the pork and cut into slices.

Melt the butter, add the onion and cook, then add the flour.

Pour over the chicken stock and white wine and stir to combine the ingredients.

The bay leaves add flavour but should be removed before serving.

COOK'S FILE

Note: Best made a day ahead to let the flavours develop. Keep in the fridge and reheat thoroughly.

VEGETARIAN MEALS

POLENTA WITH PUMPKIN AND CORN

Preparation time: 20 minutes
Total cooking time: 19 minutes
Serves 4

1 onion, roughly chopped
2 cloves garlic, crushed
1 tablespoon olive oil
300 g (9⅔ oz) pumpkin, peeled and chopped into small cubes
200 g (6½ oz) green beans, topped, tailed and cut in half
kernels from 1 corn cob
410 g (13 oz) can chopped tomatoes
1 teaspoon fresh thyme
2 teaspoons red wine vinegar
1 teaspoon finely chopped red chilli (optional)
1 cup (150 g/4¾ oz) polenta
3 cups (750 ml/24 fl oz) hot vegetable stock
50 g (1⅔ oz) butter

1 Place the onion, garlic and oil in a microwave-safe bowl. Cover and cook on High (100%) for 3 minutes.
2 Add the pumpkin, green beans, corn kernels, tomatoes, thyme, wine vinegar and chilli (if using). Stir well. Cover and cook on High (100%) for 8 minutes, stirring after 4 minutes.
3 Season to taste with salt and black pepper. Set aside in a warm place while you make the polenta.
4 Combine the polenta and stock in a microwave-safe bowl and cook on High (100%) for 8 minutes, then stir. The polenta should be soft and creamy with the consistency of mashed potatoes. If necessary, add about 100 ml/3⅓ fl oz boiling water to make the polenta a little softer. Stir in the butter and season well with salt and pepper. Serve topped with the warm vegetable sauce.

COOK'S FILE

Note: Polenta is fine golden cornmeal, served soft or left to set and then cut into wedges and grilled.
Variation: As an alternative, reduce the stock to 2½ cups (600 ml/20 fl oz), and stir in ½ cup (50 g/1⅔ oz) freshly grated Parmesan cheese instead of the butter. Spread the mixture into a foil-lined cake tin and refrigerate until firm. Cut into wedges, brush lightly with oil and grill or fry until crisp and golden brown.

Combine the pumpkin, green beans, corn, tomatoes, thyme and red wine vinegar.

Cook the polenta in stock for 8 minutes and then stir.

SOUFFLE OMELETTE WITH MUSHROOM SAUCE

Preparation time: 15 minutes
Total cooking time: 10 minutes
Serves 1–2

30 g (1 oz) butter
3 spring onions, sliced
150 g (4¾ oz) mixed mushrooms, sliced
1 tablespoon cream
3 eggs, separated
⅓ cup (40 g / 1⅓ oz) grated Cheddar cheese

1 Melt the butter in a microwave-safe bowl on High (100%) for 30 seconds. Add the spring onions and mushrooms and cook on High (100%) for 3 minutes. Stir in the cream and then season well with salt and pepper. Cook on Medium (50%) for 3 minutes, stirring every minute. Set aside.

2 In a bowl, whisk the egg yolks with 1 tablespoon water and black pepper to taste. Beat the egg whites until firm peaks form. Fold the yolk mixture into the whites. Spoon into a 20 cm (8 inch) microwave-safe pie plate. Cover and cook on High (100%) for 2 minutes.

3 Turn the omelette out onto a warmed heatproof plate, spoon the mushroom mixture onto one half and fold the other half over. Sprinkle with cheese and place under a hot grill until lightly browned—keep a close eye on it to prevent overcooking.

Cook the spring onions and mushrooms in the butter, then stir in the cream.

Fold the egg yolk mixture into the beaten egg whites, trying not to lose the volume.

Spoon the mushroom filling onto one half of the omelette. Fold the other half over.

VEGETABLE COUSCOUS

Preparation time: 20 minutes
Total cooking time: 30 minutes
Serves 4

30 g (1 oz) butter
1 onion, sliced
1 clove garlic, crushed
1 teaspoon ground cumin
2 carrots, thinly sliced
150 g (4¾ oz) pumpkin, peeled and chopped
300 g (9⅔ oz) can chickpeas, rinsed and drained
425 g (13½ oz) can chopped tomatoes
1 potato, chopped
¼ cup (60 ml/2 fl oz) vegetable stock
150 g(4¾ oz) green beans, cut into short lengths
2 zucchini, cut into chunks
1 small eggplant, chopped

Couscous
1½ cups (375 ml/12 fl oz) vegetable stock
1 cup (185 g/6 oz) couscous
30 g (1 oz) butter

1 Melt the butter in a microwave-safe bowl on High (100%) for 30 seconds. Stir in the onion, garlic and cumin. Cook on High (100%) for 3 minutes.

2 Add the carrot, pumpkin, chick peas, tomatoes, potato and vegetable stock. Cover and cook on High (100%) for 10 minutes, stirring well after 5 minutes. Mix in the beans, zucchini and eggplant. Cover and cook for 8 minutes, or until the vegetables are tender; stir well after 4 minutes. Season well with salt and pepper.

3 To make Couscous: Pour the stock and ½ cup (125 ml/4 fl oz) water into a microwave-safe bowl and heat on High (100%) for 5 minutes. Remove from the microwave and stir in the couscous. Cook on High (100%) for 3 minutes. Add the butter and toss through with a fork. Serve topped with the vegetables.

Melt the butter and then stir in the onion, garlic and cumin.

Mix in the green beans, zucchini and chopped eggplant.

Heat the stock and water, remove from the microwave and stir in the couscous.

SPICY SPLIT PEA STEW

Preparation time: 20 minutes
Total cooking time: 35 minutes
Serves 4

3/4 cup (165 g/5 1/2 oz) yellow split peas
3/4 cup (165 g/5 1/2 oz) green split peas
30 g (1 oz) butter
1 onion, finely chopped
1 clove garlic, crushed
1 teaspoon grated fresh ginger
1 teaspoon garam masala
1 teaspoon ground cumin
1 small eggplant, diced
1 potato, peeled and diced
150 g (4 3/4 oz) pumpkin, diced
3 tablespoons vegetable stock
425 g (13 1/2 oz) can chopped tomatoes

1 Wash and drain the split peas. Place in a large microwave-safe bowl and cover with boiling water. Cover; cook on High (100%) for 20 minutes, stirring after 10 minutes. Leave for 5–10 minutes; drain and set aside.

2 Melt the butter in a microwave-safe bowl on High (100%) for 30 seconds, then stir in the onion, garlic, ginger, garam masala and cumin. Cook on High (100%) for 3 minutes. Stir in the vegetables, stock and undrained tomatoes. Cover and cook on High (100%) for 10 minutes (stir after 5 and 8 minutes), until the vegetables are tender.

3 Mix together the split peas and vegetables. Season with salt and black pepper. Reheat on High (100%) for 2 minutes, stirring well after 1 minute. Serve with crusty bread.

Cook the split peas, then leave to stand for a while before draining.

Stir in the diced vegetables, stock and undrained canned tomatoes.

Mix together the split peas and vegetables and then season to taste.

PASTA SHELLS WITH SPINACH AND RICOTTA

Preparation time: 20 minutes
Total cooking time: 25 minutes
Serves 4

150 g (4¾ oz) large pasta shells
1 tablespoon oil
1 onion, chopped
1 clove garlic, crushed
2 tablespoons tomato paste
425 g (13½ oz) can chopped tomatoes
1 teaspoon dried oregano
½ teaspoon sugar
1 bunch (500 g/1 lb) English spinach
¼ cup (40 g/1⅓ oz) pine nuts
1 egg, lightly beaten
300 g (9⅔ oz) ricotta cheese
1 cup (125 g/4 oz) grated Cheddar cheese
¼ cup (35 g/1¼ oz) grated mozzarella cheese

1 Put the pasta shells in a large microwave-safe bowl, cover with boiling water and cook on High (100%) for 8 minutes, stirring twice during cooking. Leave for 5 minutes, then drain and set aside.
2 Place the oil, onion and garlic in a microwave-safe bowl and cook on High (100%) for 3 minutes. Add the tomato paste, tomatoes, oregano and sugar and cook on High (100%) for 5 minutes, stirring after 3 minutes.
3 Wash the spinach leaves and put in a microwave-safe bowl with just the water clinging to them, cover and cook on High (100%) for 2 minutes. Cool, then squeeze out the moisture and chop finely. Mix with the pine nuts, egg, ricotta and half the Cheddar cheese. Season to taste with salt and black pepper. Fill the pasta shells with the ricotta mixture.
4 Spoon a little of the tomato mixture into the base of a microwave-safe and ovenproof casserole dish. Arrange the pasta shells on top, spoon over the remaining sauce and cook on High (100%) for 5 minutes. Top with the combined mozzarella and remaining Cheddar and place under a hot grill until browned.

Cover the pasta shells generously with boiling water.

Cook the tomato mixture for 5 minutes, stirring after 3 minutes for even cooking.

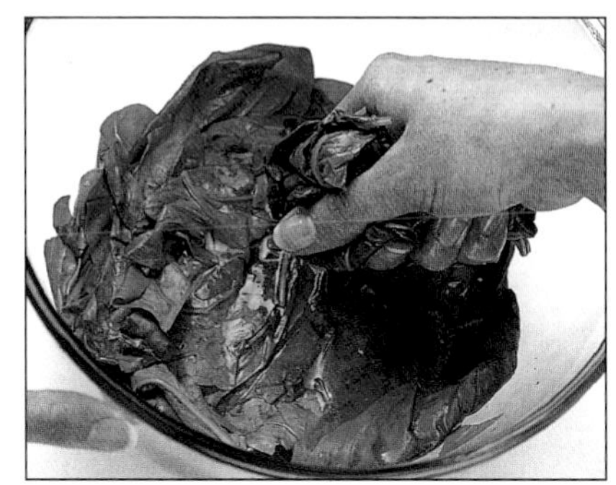

Allow the spinach to cool a little, then squeeze out any excess moisture.

Arrange the filled pasta shells on top of a little tomato sauce.

BLACK BEAN CHILLI

Preparation time: 15 minutes
Total cooking time: 1 hour 30 minutes
Serves 4–6

1 1/2 cups (330 g/10 1/2 oz) dried black beans
1 tablespoon oil
1 onion, finely chopped
1 tablespoon ground cumin
2 teaspoons ground coriander
1 teaspoon chilli powder
1/2 teaspoon ground cinnamon
2 cloves garlic, crushed
410 g (13 oz) can crushed tomatoes
1 tablespoon tomato paste
1 cup (250 ml/8 fl oz) vegetable stock

1 Place the black beans in a large microwave-safe bowl and cover with boiling water. Cover tightly and cook on High (100%) for 50 minutes. Leave for 5–10 minutes; drain and set aside.

2 Place the oil and onion in a large microwave-safe bowl and cook on High (100%) for 3 minutes. Put the cumin, coriander, chilli powder and cinnamon in a frying pan and dry-fry for 2–3 minutes, stirring until just fragrant. Add the spices and garlic to the onion mixture and cook on High (100%) for 1 minute.

3 Mix in the beans, crushed tomato, tomato paste and vegetable stock. Cook, uncovered, on High (100%) for 30 minutes, stirring every 10 minutes.

COOK'S FILE

Note: When buying black beans (also known as turtle beans) don't confuse them with Asian black beans.

Put the beans in a bowl with boiling water and cover tightly.

Dry-fry the cumin, coriander, chilli and cinnamon in a frying pan.

Mix in the black beans, crushed tomato, tomato paste and vegetable stock.

Pour boiling water over the rice and cook for 12–14 minutes.

Cook the oil and onion then stir in the curry powder and cook for 30 seconds.

Stir in the coconut milk, then add the vegetables and cook.

When the rice is reheated, fluff it up with a fork to break up any clumps.

CREAMY VEGETABLE CURRY WITH RICE

Preparation time: 30 minutes
Total cooking time: 30 minutes
Serves 2

1½ cups (300 g/9⅔ oz) white rice
½ teaspoon salt
1 tablespoon vegetable oil
1 onion, finely chopped
1 tablespoon curry powder
1 cup (250 ml/8 fl oz) coconut milk
90 g (3 oz) broccoli, cut into florets
125 g (4 oz) beans, cut into short lengths
1 carrot, cut into cubes
250 g (8 oz) pumpkin, cut into small cubes

1 Place the rice in a large microwave-safe bowl with 3 cups (750 ml/24 fl oz) boiling water and the salt. Cook on High (100%) for 12–14 minutes. (Do not cover or the rice will boil over.) Set aside.

2 Place the oil and onion in a large microwave-safe dish and cook on High (100%) for 2 minutes. Stir in the curry powder and cook on High (100%) for 30 seconds.

3 Pour the coconut milk into the dish and stir so that it is well combined. Add the vegetables, cover and cook on High (100%) for 10 minutes; stir after 5 minutes.

4 Reheat the rice on High (100%) for 2 minutes and fluff up with a fork. Serve the curry over the rice.

COOK'S FILE

Note: Rice cooks very well in advance. After rinsing with hot water, cover and refrigerate until required. If you are using brown rice, follow the same instructions for reheating, but cook the rice initially for 25 minutes.

MUSHROOM AND ZUCCHINI TERRINE

Preparation time: 10 minutes + 4 hours chilling
Total cooking time:10 minutes
Serves 6–8

250 g (8 oz) zucchini
250 g (8 oz) button mushrooms
100 g (3 1/3 oz) butter
4 cloves garlic, crushed
1 teaspoon fresh thyme leaves
1 teaspoon cumin seeds
1 cup (250 g/8 oz) whole egg mayonnaise
2 teaspoons gelatine

1 Thinly slice the zucchini and the button mushrooms, then set aside in separate bowls.
2 In a microwave-safe bowl melt half the butter for 30 seconds on High (100%). Add half the garlic and cook for 30 seconds on High (100%). Add the zucchini and thyme and cook on High (100%) for 4 minutes. Set aside to cool.
3 In a microwave-safe bowl melt the remaining butter for 30 seconds on High (100%). Add the remaining garlic and cook on High (100%) for 30 seconds. Add the mushrooms and cumin seeds and cook on High (100%) for 3 minutes. Set aside to cool.
4 To each bowl of vegetable mixture add 1/2 cup (125 g/4 oz) mayonnaise and salt and pepper to taste. Stir well.
5 Sprinkle the gelatine over 2 tablespoons water in a small bowl, then cook on High (100%) for 30 seconds until fully dissolved. Stir to ensure the gelatine is dissolved. Cool slightly, then pour half the gelatine into each bowl of vegetable mixture. Mix well.
6 Spoon the zucchini mixture into the base of a 3-cup (750 ml/24 fl oz) bar tin or terrine mould, smooth and spoon over the mushroom mixture. Cover and chill for at least 4 hours, or until the terrine has set firm. When ready to serve, loosen the edges of the terrine with a sharp knife and turn out onto a serving plate. Slice with a serrated knife and serve with bread.

COOK'S FILE

Note: Will keep, covered, for up to 2 days in the refrigerator.

Thinly slice the zucchini and mushrooms and place in separate bowls.

Put 2 tablespoons water in a small bowl and sprinkle with the gelatine.

Spoon the zucchini mixture into the tin, then spoon over the mushroom mixture.

Before turning out, loosen the edges of the terrine with a sharp knife.

SAFFRON RISOTTO

Preparation time: 15 minutes
Total cooking time: 22 minutes
Serves 4

1/4 teaspoon saffron threads
30 g (1 oz) butter
1 onion, finely chopped
1 cup (220 g/7 oz) arborio rice
3 cups (750 ml/24 fl oz) vegetable stock
1/2 cup (50 g/1 2/3 oz) grated Parmesan

1 Soak the saffron threads in a tablespoon of warm water. Melt the butter in a microwave-safe bowl on High (100%) for 30 seconds. Stir in the onion and cook on High (100%) for 2 minutes. Stir in the rice until well coated with butter. Cook on High (100%) for 1 minute.

2 Add the stock and saffron threads with their water and cook on High (100%) for 10 minutes. Remove from the microwave and stir well. Return to the microwave and cook on High (100%) for a further 8 minutes.

3 Stir in the Parmesan cheese and season well with salt and pepper. Leave for 5 minutes before serving so the rice can absorb any excess liquid.

COOK'S FILE

Storage time: Risotto should be served immediately as it does not keep well.

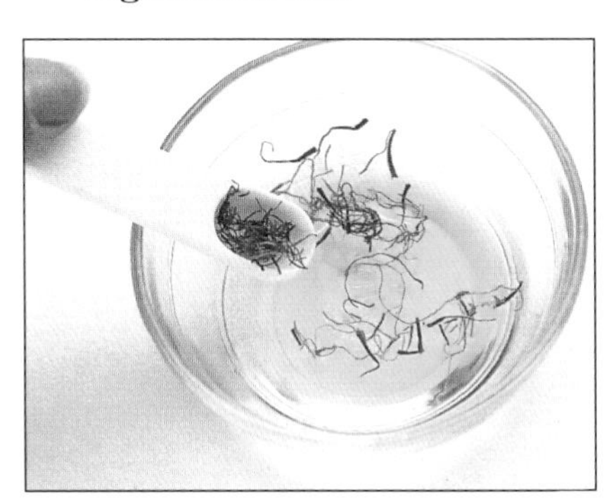

Soak the saffron threads in 1 tablespoon of warm water.

Add the rice and stir until well coated with butter.

Cook for 10 minutes, then remove from the oven and stir. Cook for 8 minutes.

EGGPLANT PARMIGIANA

Preparation time: 30 minutes
Total cooking time: 22 minutes
Serves 4

1 tablespoon olive oil
4 large tomatoes, peeled, seeded and chopped
2 cloves garlic, crushed
1 tablespoon tomato paste
1 teaspoon dried oregano leaves
1 teaspoon sugar
8 black olives, pitted and chopped
2 medium eggplants
1½ cups (225 g/7¼ oz) grated mozzarella cheese

1 Heat the olive oil in a large microwave-safe bowl for 1 minute on High (100%). Add the tomatoes, garlic, tomato paste, oregano, sugar and olives and cook on High (100%) for 8 minutes, stirring after 4 minutes.

2 Thinly slice the eggplants and place half in a shallow microwave-safe and ovenproof dish. Top with half the tomato sauce, then another layer of eggplant, then the remaining tomato sauce. Cover loosely and cook on High (100%) for 10 minutes.

3 Sprinkle with mozzarella and put under a hot grill until the cheese turns golden brown. Garnish with fresh oregano leaves, if available.

COOK'S FILE

Note: To peel tomatoes, score a cross in the base, plunge into boiling water then into cold and peel away the skin.

Add the tomatoes, garlic, tomato paste, dried oregano, sugar and olives.

Top the layer of eggplant with half the tomato sauce, then more eggplant.

Sprinkle with grated mozzarella and then brown under a hot grill.

PASTA WITH SPRING VEGETABLES

Preparation time: 15 minutes
Total cooking time: 25 minutes
Serves 4

500 g (1 lb) spaghetti
150 g (4¾ oz) broccoli florets
155 g (5 oz) asparagus, cut into short lengths
200 g (6½ oz) frozen broad beans, thawed and peeled
1 cup (155 g/5 oz) frozen peas
30 g (1 oz) butter
1 onion, finely chopped
1 cup (250 ml/8 fl oz) cream
½ cup (50 g/1⅔ oz) grated Parmesan

1 Place the spaghetti in a large microwave-safe bowl, cover with plenty of boiling water and cook on High (100%) for 10 minutes, stirring twice during cooking. Leave for 5 minutes, then drain and set aside.

2 Arrange the broccoli florets around the outside of a shallow microwave-safe dish. Put the asparagus in the middle and sprinkle with a little water. Cover and cook on High (100%) for 5 minutes. Remove from the dish and set aside.

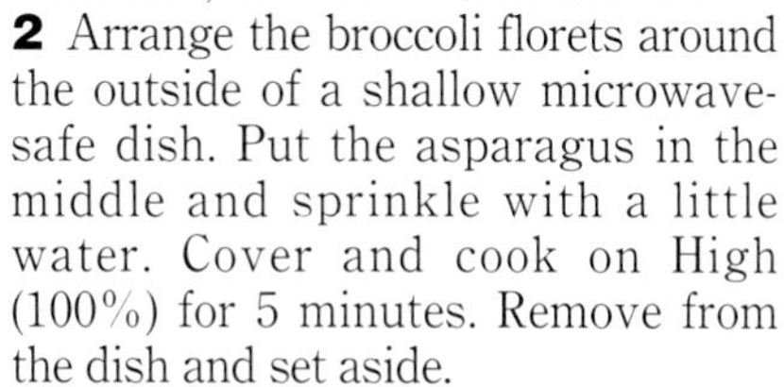

3 Arrange the beans around the outside of the dish and the peas in the centre. Sprinkle with water, cover and cook on High (100%) for 3 minutes.

4 In a large microwave-safe bowl, melt the butter on High (100%) for 30 seconds. Stir in the onion and cook on High (100%) for 3 minutes. Stir in the cream and cheese and heat on Medium (50%) for 3 minutes. Stir in the vegetables and toss through the pasta. Reheat for 2 minutes on Medium (50%). Season to taste and serve with shavings of Parmesan.

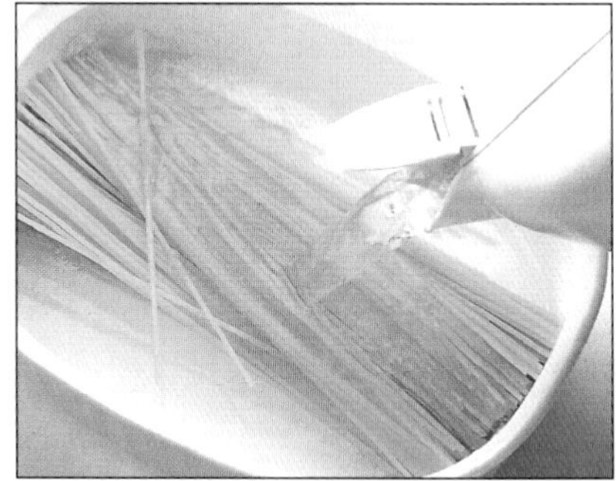

Put the pasta in a large bowl and cover generously with boiling water.

Arrange the broccoli florets around the outside of the dish so they cook evenly.

The broad beans are denser than the peas so arrange them on the outside.

Cook the onion in the butter, then stir in the cream and cheese.

COOK'S FILE

Note: The best quality Parmesan is Parmigiano Reggiano. Buy it in blocks and grate as required.

Jams and Chutneys

We all love jams and chutneys but the thought of making them at home conjures up images of huge pots bubbling on the stove for days on end. Think again—the microwave oven can produce delicious full-flavoured preserves with the minimum of fuss and mess, and all in a matter of minutes.

There are a few simple rules to follow when making jams and chutneys in the microwave. The first is to check the mixture frequently while cooking. If it looks as if it is going to boil over, stop the microwave and let the mixture settle, then resume cooking. To test that it has reached setting point, place a teaspoonful onto a plate, then put it in the freezer for a minute. Run a spoon through the mixture: if it holds a line it is ready. If not, cook for a further 2 minutes before retesting. Place the hot jam into sterilised jars, seal and store in a cool, dark place for up to 4 months. Refrigerate after opening.

CITRUS MARMALADE

Chop 1 lemon, 1 lime and 1 orange, removing the seeds. Place in a food processor and process roughly. Place into a large deep microwave-safe glass bowl with 1½ cups (375 ml/12 fl oz) water. Cover with plastic wrap and cook on High (100%) for 10 minutes. Cool slightly, then measure the volume. Add 1 cup (250 g/8 oz) sugar for every cup of fruit mixture and stir until the sugar is dissolved. Cook on High (100%), uncovered, for 18 minutes, until the mixture reaches setting point. Makes 3 cups (750 ml/24 fl oz).

GRAPE JAM

Take 500 g (1 lb) green grapes, cut the grapes in half and remove the seeds if necessary. Place in a large deep microwave-safe glass bowl with 1⅓ cups (340 g/10¾ oz) sugar, 2 tablespoons water and 2 teaspoons lemon juice. Cook on High (100%) for 18 minutes, stirring every 5 minutes, until the mixture has reached setting point. Makes 1½ cups (375 ml/12 fl oz).

STRAWBERRY JAM

Mix 500 g (1 lb) halved strawberries together with 1⅓ cups (340 g/10¾ oz) sugar in a large deep microwave-safe glass bowl and leave for 10 minutes. Add 1 tablespoon lemon juice and cook on High (100%) for 18 minutes, stirring every 6 minutes, until the mixture reaches setting point. Makes about 1½ cups (375 ml/12 fl oz).

MANGO CHUTNEY

Peel, stone and chop 3 large mangoes. Place in a bowl with ½ cup (125 ml/4 fl oz) white wine vinegar and ½ cup (95 g/3¼ oz) soft brown sugar, 2 teaspoons grated fresh ginger, 6 cloves, 1 small grated onion and ½ teaspoon each of salt and finely chopped red chilli. Cook on High (100%) for 9 minutes, stirring once. Remove from the microwave and mash roughly with a fork. Pour into sterilised jars and keep in a cool dark place for up to 6 weeks. Refrigerate after opening. Makes about 4 cups (1 litre).

TOMATO RELISH

Score small crosses in the bases of 8 tomatoes and place in a heatproof bowl. Cover with boiling water, leave for 3 minutes then plunge into cold water and peel the skin away from the cross. Remove the seeds and roughly chop the flesh. Put in a large microwave-safe bowl with 1 finely chopped onion. Cook on High (100%) for 7 minutes. Add 3 teaspoons of salt, 1 teaspoon each of paprika and chopped red chilli and ¼ cup (60 ml/2 fl oz) white wine vinegar and cook on High (100%) for 5 minutes. Stir in ⅔ cup (125 g/4 oz) soft brown sugar and cook on High (100%) for a further 5 minutes. Pour into sterilised jars and store in a cool, dark place for up to 6 weeks. Refrigerate after opening. Makes about 4 cups (1 litre).

From left: Citrus Marmalade; Grape Jam; Strawberry Jam; Mango Chutney; Tomato Relish

DESSERTS

CREME BRULEE

Preparation time: 15 minutes + chilling
Total cooking time: 14 minutes
Serves 6

2¼ cups (560 ml/18 fl oz) cream
4 egg yolks
3 tablespoons sugar
2 teaspoons vanilla essence

Toffee
4 tablespoons sugar

1 Place the cream in a microwave-safe jug and heat on High (100%) for 3 minutes. Meanwhile, in a microwave-safe bowl, whisk together the egg yolks, sugar and vanilla. Pour over the warmed cream, stirring all the time.

2 Cook the mixture on Medium (50%) for 3 minutes 30 seconds, stirring every 1 minute. The mixture should now be a thickened custard (test by dipping a spoon in it: you should be able to draw a line down the back with your finger).

3 Pour the custard into six ½-cup (125 ml/4 fl oz) ramekins and chill for at least 3 hours. Make the brulée just before you are ready to serve.

4 To make Toffee: Remove the chilled custards from the fridge and place close to the microwave. Place the sugar and ⅓ cup (80 ml/2¾ fl oz) water in a glass microwave-safe jug. Cook on High (100%) for 7 minutes. Remove quickly from the microwave and pour about 1 tablespoon of toffee over each chilled custard. (You need to work quickly as the toffee carries on cooking in the jug even when out of the microwave.) Take great care when handling the hot toffee. Keep it well away from children. Serve the Crème Brulées immediately.

Pour the warmed cream into the egg yolk mixture, stirring continuously.

When the custard is thickened you can draw a line through it on the spoon.

Transfer the custard to a jug and pour into six ramekins.

Quickly pour the hot toffee over the chilled custards, so it hardens instantly.

STICKY DATE PUDDINGS

Preparation time: 25 minutes
Total cooking time: 18 minutes
Serves 6

185 g (6 oz) fresh dates, pitted and chopped
300 ml (9½ fl oz) water
1 teaspoon bicarbonate of soda
70 g (2⅓ oz) butter, melted
185 g (6 oz) raw sugar
¼ teaspoon vanilla essence
2 eggs, lightly beaten
185 g (6 oz) self-raising flour

Sauce
300 g (9⅔ oz) soft brown sugar
1 cup (250 ml/8 fl oz) cream
60 g (2 oz) butter
1 teaspoon vanilla essence

1 Brush two 6-hole microwave muffin trays with melted butter. Place the dates and water in a large bowl and cook on High (100%) for 6 minutes. Mash the dates with a fork until pulpy. Stir in the bicarbonate of soda until foamy. Set aside to cool slightly. Stir in the butter.
2 Add the sugar and vanilla essence and mix well. Add the eggs gradually, beating well after each addition. Using a metal spoon, fold in the sifted flour. Stir until just combined—take care not to overbeat.
3 Spoon the mixture into the muffin trays and cook on Medium High (75%) for 6 minutes. Leave to stand for 3–4 minutes before serving.
4 To make Sauce: Combine the sugar, cream, butter and vanilla essence in a microwave-safe bowl and cook on High (100%) for 5 minutes 30 seconds, stirring well after every minute. Turn the puddings out and serve immediately with hot sauce. Delicious with cream or ice cream.

COOK'S FILE

Hint: If you do not have microwave muffin trays, you can cook the puddings in eight ½-cup (125 ml/4 fl oz) microwave-safe ramekins. These should be cooked on Medium High (75%) for 9 minutes 30 seconds.
Note: Raw sugar is the dark sticky mass of sugar and molasses made by boiling down cane sugar juice.

Stir in the bicarbonate of soda until the mixture becomes foamy.

Using a metal spoon, fold in the sifted flour. Stir to combine but don't overbeat.

Spoon the mixture into the muffin trays and cook for 6 minutes.

Cook the sauce on High, stirring well after every minute.

RICE PUDDING

Preparation time: 10 minutes
Total cooking time: 30 minutes
Serves 2–4

1/2 cup (110 g/3 2/3 oz) short-grain rice
2 cups (500 ml/16 fl oz) milk
200 ml (6 1/2 fl oz) cream
3 tablespoons sugar
pinch of freshly grated nutmeg
sprinkle of cinnamon, to garnish

1 Place the rice, half the milk, the cream, sugar and nutmeg in a large microwave-safe bowl. Cook on High (100%) for 8 minutes and then stir.

2 Add the remaining milk and then cook on Medium (50%) for a further 19 minutes.

3 Leave the rice pudding to stand for at least 10 minutes before serving (this makes it even creamier). Reheat for 2 minutes on High (100%), then sprinkle with cinnamon and serve.

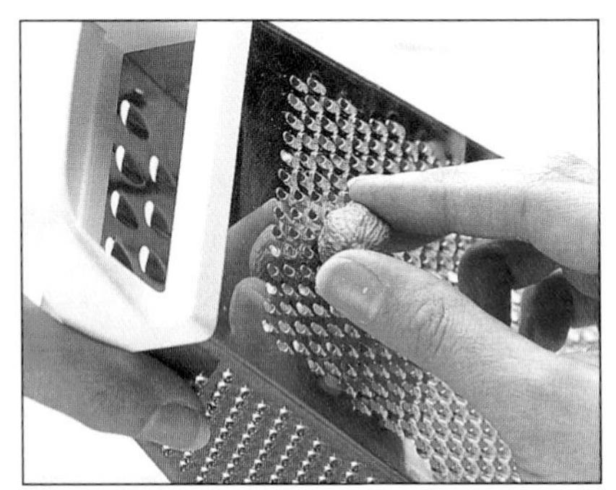

It is worth buying fresh nutmeg for its far superior flavour.

Place the rice, half the milk, the cream, sugar and nutmeg in a bowl.

Add the remaining milk and cook for another 19 minutes.

MANGO ICE CREAM

Preparation time: 10 minutes + freezing
Total cooking time: 14 minutes
Serves 4–6

3 cups (750 ml/24 fl oz) cream
1 cup (250 ml/8 fl oz) full-cream milk
3/4 cup (185 g/6 oz) sugar
4 egg yolks
2 large mangoes (or 250 g/8 oz frozen mango purée)

1 Place the cream and milk in a large microwave-safe jug or bowl and heat on High (100%) for 3 minutes.

2 In a large microwave-safe bowl, whisk together the sugar and egg yolks until well mixed, then slowly add the warmed cream and milk. Cook on Medium (50%) for 11 minutes; stir every 2 minutes. The mixture should have thickened to coat the back of a spoon. Cool, then refrigerate to chill.

3 Remove the skin and stones of the mangoes and mash the flesh with a fork. Fold into the chilled ice cream, then freeze in a metal container, covered with foil. When partially frozen, beat with electric beaters, then refreeze completely.

COOK'S FILE

Note: If your ice cream appears very hard before serving, take it out of the freezer half an hour before required.

Slowly add the warmed cream and milk to the mixture of sugar and egg yolks.

When the mixture has thickened you will be able to draw a line through it.

Beat the partially frozen mixture and then refreeze.

Be sure to stop and stir the chocolate, even though it may not look melted.

Use a metal spoon to gently fold through the egg whites.

Use a small brush to paint the melted chocolate onto the leaves.

If the chocolate coating is too thin it will break when the leaf is peeled away.

RICH CHOCOLATE MOUSSE WITH CHOCOLATE LEAVES

Preparation time: 30 minutes + chilling
Total cooking time: 5 minutes
Serves 6

300 g (9 2/3 oz) dark chocolate
5 eggs, separated
2 tablespoons Cognac
2 cups (500 ml/16 fl oz) cream
2 tablespoons sugar
50 g (1 2/3 oz) dark compound chocolate
cocoa powder, to dust

1 Break up the dark chocolate and place in a microwave-safe bowl. Melt on Medium (50%) for 3–4 minutes and stir. (The chocolate will melt in the shape of the blocks, so stir even though it might not look completely melted.) Cool slightly. Whisk the egg yolks and Cognac into the chocolate.
2 Beat the cream and sugar with electric beaters until stiff peaks form. Whisk the egg whites until stiff peaks form. Fold the cream mixture into the chocolate mixture with a metal spoon, then fold in the egg whites, trying not to deflate them too much. Pour into a serving bowl or individual bowls and refrigerate until set.
3 To make Chocolate Leaves: Choose a selection of small leaves such as camellia, ivy or rose and wipe clean with a damp cloth. Place the compound chocolate in a microwave-safe bowl and melt on Medium (50%) for 1–1 1/2 minutes.
4 Paint the chocolate onto the leaves with a small brush. Leave in a cool place until set and then carefully peel away the leaves. Garnish the Mousses with the chocolate leaves and dust liberally with cocoa powder.

COOK'S FILE

Note: The leaves can be prepared well in advance: just store them in a small container in the refrigerator.

Quick and Easy Desserts

LEMON CURD CREAM

To make Lemon Curd: Combine 3 egg yolks, 3 tablespoons caster sugar, 50 g (1⅔ oz) melted butter, 2 tablespoons lemon juice and 2 teaspoons finely grated lemon rind in a microwave-safe bowl. Whisk until the sugar dissolves. Cook on Medium (50%) for 1 minute, then whisk well. Cook for a further 1 minute 30 seconds, whisking every 30 seconds. Take care that the mixture doesn't overcook and curdle. Cool completely. Whip 3 tablespoons cream until soft peaks form, then fold gently into the lemon curd. Serve with fresh fruit and dessert biscuits. Serves 4.

HOT FUDGE SAUCE

Combine 200 g (6½ oz) chopped dark chocolate and ½ cup (125 ml/4 fl oz) cream in a microwave-safe bowl. Cook on Medium (50%) for 2 minutes, stirring well after 1 minute. Stir in 1 tablespoon rum or brandy, if liked, and serve over ice cream and fresh fruit. Serves 6.

BLUEBERRY TOPPING

Combine 200 g (6½ oz) blueberries, 1 teaspoon finely grated lemon rind, 2 teaspoons lemon juice and 1 tablespoon icing sugar in a microwave-safe bowl. Cook on High (100%) for 2 minutes, stirring after 1 minute. Serve hot or cold, over ice cream, waffles or pancakes. Serves 4.

Clockwise from left: Lemon Curd Cream; Hot Fudge Sauce; Boozy Figs; Rum Bananas; Wine-poached Pears; Blueberry Topping

BOOZY FIGS

Combine 1 cup (250 ml/8 fl oz) fresh orange juice, 1 tablespoon sugar and 1 tablespoon orange-flavoured liqueur in a bowl and cook on High (100%) for 2 minutes. Stir in 12 whole dried figs and cook on High (100%) for 5 minutes, stirring after 3 minutes, until the figs are soft and plump. Serve warm with thick cream. Serves 4.

RUM BANANAS

Melt 50 g (1⅔ oz) butter in a microwave-safe jug on High (100%) for 30 seconds, then add 2 tablespoons soft brown sugar, ¼ cup orange juice and 2 tablespoons rum and stir to combine. Peel 4 bananas, cut in half lengthways, then halve again and place in a shallow microwave-safe dish. Pour the butter mixture over the bananas, cover loosely with plastic wrap and cook on High (100%) for 3 minutes 30 seconds. Serve warm with cream or ice cream. Serves 4.

WINE-POACHED PEARS

Combine 2½ cups (600 ml/20 fl oz) good-quality red wine, 5 cups (1.25 litres) water, 1 cinnamon stick, a wide piece of lemon rind (white pith removed) and 3 whole cloves in a deep microwave-safe bowl. Cook on High (100%) for 10 minutes. Peel 4 pears, keeping the stems intact. Place in the wine mixture and cook on High (100%) for 20 minutes, stirring every 5 minutes. Serve the pears warm or at room temperature, with a little of the liquid. Serves 4.

POACHED PLUMS WITH MASCARPONE CREAM AND TOFFEE

Preparation time: 20 minutes
Total cooking time: 12 minutes
Serves 4

1.5 kg (3 lb) fresh ripe plums
1/4 cup (60 ml/2 fl oz) apple juice
1/4 cup (60 g/2 oz) sugar
1 teaspoon vanilla essence

Mascarpone Cream
1/2 cup (125 ml/4 fl oz) cream, whipped
125 g (4 oz) mascarpone
icing sugar, to taste

Toffee
4 tablespoons sugar

1 Pierce the plums with a small sharp knife and place in a microwave-safe bowl. Add the apple juice, sugar and vanilla essence and cook on High (100%) for 5 minutes. Cool, cut in half and remove the skins and stones.

2 To make Mascarpone Cream: Fold the whipped cream into the mascarpone and add icing sugar to taste. Arrange the poached plums in four individual heatproof dishes and top with Mascarpone Cream.

3 To make Toffee: Place the sugar and 1/3 cup (80 ml/2 3/4 fl oz) water in a glass microwave-safe jug. Cook on High (100%) for 7 minutes until the mixture turns to caramel. Working very quickly (as the mixture carries on cooking in the jug) pour about a tablespoon of toffee over each portion of mascarpone. Serve immediately.

Allow the plums to cool, then cut in half and remove the skins and stones.

Fold the cream into the mascarpone and add sugar to taste.

To make toffee, cook the sugar and water for 7 minutes.

CHOCOLATE PUDDINGS WITH CREME ANGLAISE

Preparation time: 20 minutes
Total cooking time: 11 minutes
Serves 6

75 g (2½ oz) butter
125 g (4 oz) dark chocolate, chopped
150 ml (4¾ fl oz) milk
50 g (1⅔ oz) caster sugar
2 eggs, separated
½ teaspoon vanilla essence
1 cup (80 g/2⅔ oz) fresh white breadcrumbs

Crème Anglaise
300 ml (9½ fl oz) cream
2 egg yolks
½ teaspoon vanilla essence
1 tablespoon caster sugar

1 Melt the butter and chocolate in a microwave-safe bowl on High (100%) for 1½ minutes. Warm the milk in a microwave-safe jug on High (100%) for 1 minute, then add to the chocolate mixture. Stir in the sugar, lightly beaten egg yolks and vanilla essence until smooth. Stir in the breadcrumbs.

2 Whisk the egg whites until stiff and gently fold into the mixture. Pour into six greased ½-cup (125 ml/4 fl oz) microwave-safe ramekins or cups. Place around the outside of the microwave turntable and cook on High (100%) for 4 minutes. Leave for a few minutes before turning out.

3 To make Crème Anglaise: Put the cream, egg yolks, vanilla essence and caster sugar in a large microwave-safe bowl and whisk together. Cook on Medium (50%) for 4 minutes 30 seconds, stirring after 3 minutes and then every 30 seconds. The custard should thicken enough to coat the back of a spoon. Serve with the steamed chocolate puddings. Delicious topped with shavings or curls of dark chocolate.

Stir in the sugar, egg yolks and vanilla essence, then stir in the breadcrumbs.

Place the puddings around the outside of the microwave turntable.

Whisk together the cream, egg yolks, vanilla essence and caster sugar.

BAKED APPLES

Preparation time: 20 minutes
Total cooking time: 10 minutes
Serves 4

4 green apples
2 tablespoons finely chopped sultanas
2 tablespoons finely chopped dried apricots
30 g (1 oz) butter, melted
1 teaspoon ground cinnamon

1 Core the apples, leaving the skins on. Slice each apple horizontally into 4 slices. Reassemble the slices to form whole apples.
2 Mix together the chopped sultanas and apricots, butter and cinnamon. Divide the filling mixture into four and stuff, using your fingers, into the cored apples.
3 Place the apples in a microwave-safe dish and cover loosely. Cook on High (100%) for 10 minutes. Leave for 5 minutes before serving, drizzled with the cooking juices. Delicious with custard or whipped cream.

Core the apples and then slice horizontally into four pieces.

Use your fingers to stuff the filling into the cored apples.

Put the apples in a dish and cover loosely with microwave wrap.

Allow the apple to cool, then mash with a fork and add honey to taste.

Fold together the yoghurt and whipped cream and layer over the apple.

Fry the breadcrumbs in the butter—they may stick together at first.

Remove the pan from the heat and stir the sugar into the cooled breadcrumbs.

CRUNCHY CINNAMON APPLE PUDDING

Preparation time: 20 minutes
Total cooking time: 10 minutes
Serves 4

4 green apples, peeled, cored and roughly chopped
1/4 teaspoon ground cinnamon
honey, to taste
200 g (6 1/2 oz) natural yoghurt
200 ml (6 1/2 fl oz) cream, whipped
50 g (1 2/3 oz) butter
1 cup (80 g/2 2/3 oz) fresh breadcrumbs
2 tablespoons soft brown sugar

1 Place the apple and cinnamon in a microwave-safe bowl and loosely cover. Cook for 7 minutes on High (100%), stirring after 5 minutes. (The apple should be soft and fully cooked.) Leave to cool, mash with a fork and add honey to taste. Place in a serving dish or individual dishes.

2 Fold together the yoghurt and whipped cream and layer on top of the apple mixture. Refrigerate.

3 Melt the butter in a small frying pan and add the fresh breadcrumbs. Gently cook, stirring, until the crumbs are golden and crunchy. (The breadcrumbs will stick together at first, and separate as they cook.) Allow to cool.

4 Add the brown sugar to the breadcrumbs and then sprinkle over the yoghurt and cream and serve.

COOK'S FILE

Hint: This dessert looks attractive served in glass bowls so that all the different layers can be seen.

Hot Toddies

MULLED WINE

In a large microwave-safe jug, mix together 2 cups (500 ml/16 fl oz) good-quality red wine, 3/4 cup (185 ml/6 fl oz) orange juice, 1/4 cup (60 ml/2 fl oz) brandy, 3 cloves, 1 cinnamon stick, 1 teaspoon freshly grated ginger, 1 wide piece of lemon rind (white pith removed) and 1 tablespoon honey. Heat on High (100%) for 8 minutes, then strain and serve warm, garnished with thin slices of orange and lemon. Serves 4.

Clockwise from left: Mulled Wine; Mocha Coffee; Cafe Latte; Hot Rum Punch; Hot Chocolate; Liqueur Coffee

MOCHA COFFEE

Put 1 1/2 cups (375 ml/12 fl oz) milk in a large jug and heat on High (100%) for 2 1/2 minutes. Add 1/2 cup (125 ml/4 fl oz) hot black coffee and 2 teaspoons powdered drinking chocolate and stir to combine. Pour into cups, top with whipped cream and sprinkle with extra drinking chocolate. Serves 2.

LIQUEUR COFFEE

To make Liqueur Coffee, make as for the Mocha Coffee, but substitute your favourite liqueur for the drinking chocolate. You will need about 1 tablespoon of liqueur for 1 1/2 cups (375 ml/12 fl oz) of milk, or to taste. Use dark rum for Jamaican coffee, whiskey for Irish coffee and Kahlua for Mexican coffee.

CAFE LATTE

Place 1 cup (250 ml/8 fl oz) milk in a microwave-safe jug and heat on High (100%) for 3 minutes. Stir in 1 cup (250 ml/8 fl oz) hot strong black coffee and add sugar to taste. Reheat if necessary and serve immediately. Serves 2.

HOT CHOCOLATE

Place 2 cups (500 ml/16 fl oz) milk and 60 g (2 oz) grated dark chocolate in a large microwave-safe jug. Heat on High (100%) for 4 minutes, until the chocolate has melted. Stir to fully combine, then heat for another minute. Stir in 2 chopped marshmallows and 1/2 teaspoon vanilla essence. Serve immediately. Serves 2.

HOT RUM PUNCH

Heat 2 cups (500 ml/16 fl oz) water in a microwave-safe jug on High (100%) for 3 minutes. Add 2 teaspoons tea leaves, 1 cinnamon stick and 4 cloves and set aside for 5 minutes then strain. Combine 1/2 cup (125 ml/4 fl oz) each of rum, white wine and orange juice in another microwave-safe jug, and heat for 4 minutes on High (100%). Add this to the tea mixture and reheat briefly. Serve immediately with a slice of orange in each glass. Serves 4.

CHOCOLATE CHEESECAKE

Preparation time: 20 minutes + chilling
Total cooking time: 3 minutes
Serves 6

200 g (6½ oz) chocolate-flavoured biscuits
100 g (3⅓ oz) butter

Filling
¾ cup (185 ml/6 fl oz) cream
250 g (8 oz) light cream cheese
3 tablespoons caster sugar
100 g (3⅓ oz) dark chocolate
3 teaspoons gelatine
chocolate flakes, broken into pieces

1 Grease and line the base of a 20 cm (8 inch) springform tin or tart dish with a loose base. Process the biscuits into fine crumbs in a food processor. Melt the butter in a microwave-safe jug for 1 minute on High (100%) then mix with the crumbs. Press the crumb mixture into the base and side of the tin or tart dish and refrigerate.
2 To make Filling: Pour the cream into the food processor and process for 1 minute, or until thickened. Add the light cream cheese and sugar and process in short bursts to combine. Place the chocolate in a microwave-safe jug and melt on Medium (50%) for 2 minutes, then stir. Allow to cool.
3 Sprinkle the gelatine over 3 tablespoons water and microwave on High (100%) for 30 seconds so that it is fully dissolved. Stir well with a fork. Spoon the melted chocolate and the dissolved gelatine into the food processor and process until well combined with the cream and cheese.
4 Pour the filling onto the biscuit base and refrigerate for a few hours to set. Before serving, remove from the tin or tart dish and decorate with chocolate flake. Good served with fresh berries.

COOK'S FILE

Hint: Cream cheese is easier to work with if you leave it to soften at room temperature first.
Note: When melting chocolate make sure you check it after the stated time—it melts in blocks.

Press the crumb base firmly into the tin with the back of a spoon.

Add the cream cheese and sugar to the whipped cream and process.

Stir the heated gelatine with a fork to make sure it is fully dissolved.

Pour the chocolate filling over the base and refrigerate until set.

BREAD AND BUTTER PUDDING

Preparation time: 15 minutes
Total cooking time: 14 minutes
Serves 4

6 slices fruit loaf
30 g (1 oz) butter
2 cups (500 ml/16 fl oz)milk
1 vanilla bean, cut in half
4 egg yolks
3 tablespoons caster sugar
2 tablespoons demerara sugar
1/4 teaspoon ground nutmeg

1 Spread both sides of the bread with butter. Halve each slice diagonally and arrange in a 5-cup (1.25 litre) microwave-safe and heatproof dish.
2 Place the milk and vanilla bean in a microwave-safe jug and heat on High (100%) for 4 minutes. Remove the vanilla bean, scraping out the seeds. Whisk together the yolks and sugar; gradually whisk in the hot milk.
3 Pour the custard mixture over the bread, then sprinkle with demerara sugar and nutmeg. Cook on Medium High (75%) for 10 minutes. Leave for 10 minutes before serving, to allow the custard to cook completely.

COOK'S FILE

Variation: Brown the pudding briefly under a hot grill but don't let the custard overcook and break down.
Note: Vanilla beans can be dried out and re-used. You can use 1 teaspoon vanilla essence instead, but add it once the custard is made.

Butter the bread on both sides and cut each slice in half diagonally.

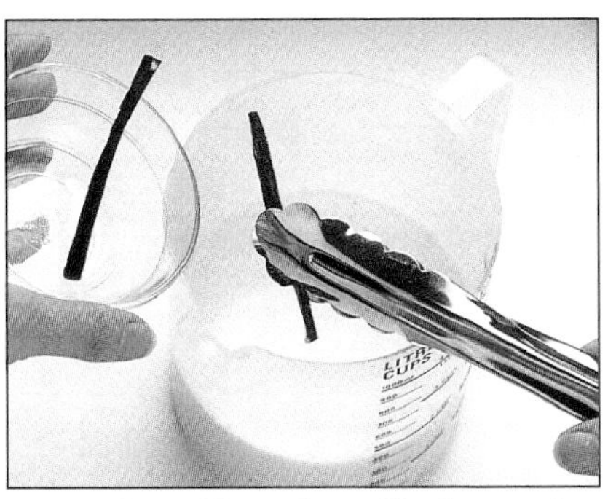

Heat the milk and vanilla bean, then remove the bean.

Pour the custard over the bread, then sprinkle with sugar and nutmeg.

PEAR CRUMBLE

Preparation time: 10 minutes
Total cooking time: 15 minutes
Serves 4

4 firm pears
1 cup (125 g/4 oz) plain flour
100 g (3 1/3 oz) butter
1/2 cup (95 g/3 1/4 oz) soft brown sugar

1 Peel the pears and slice into quarters. Remove the core, then cut into thin slices. Pack firmly into a 5 cup (1.25 litre) capacity microwave-safe and ovenproof dish. Sprinkle with 1 tablespoon of water.

2 Rub together the flour and butter until crumbly, then mix in the sugar. (This can be done in a food processor.)

3 Sprinkle the crumble mixture over the pears and cook on High (100%) for 15 minutes. Every 5 minutes lightly brush the crumb mixture with a fork to prevent it sticking together and to ensure even cooking. If you want to brown the topping further, place the dish under a hot grill for 2 minutes. Serve with cream or custard.

COOK'S FILE

Variation: Use 6 fresh peaches instead of pears. Skin the peaches by leaving in boiling water for 4 minutes. Slice and then continue as for pears.

Peel the pears, cut into quarters and slice thinly, removing the core.

Rub together the flour and butter with your fingertips until crumbly.

Lightly brush the crumb mixture with a fork to prevent it sticking together.

RHUBARB FOOL WITH BRANDY SNAPS

Preparation time: 30 minutes + chilling
Total cooking time: 11 minutes
Serves 4

400 g (12$\frac{2}{3}$ oz) rhubarb (about 12 sticks), chopped
4 tablespoons caster sugar
1 cup (250 ml/8 fl oz) cream
1 cup (250 ml/8 fl oz) ready-made custard

Brandy Snaps
30 g (1 oz) butter
1 tablespoon golden syrup
2 tablespoons soft brown sugar
$\frac{1}{2}$ teaspoon ground ginger
2 tablespoons plain flour

1 Place the rhubarb and sugar in a microwave-safe bowl; loosely cover. Cook on High (100%) for 4 minutes. Purée in a food processor until smooth and then cool. Beat the cream until soft peaks form. Fold the cream and custard into the rhubarb purée. Pour into a serving bowl and refrigerate for a few hours.

2 To make Brandy Snaps: Place the butter, syrup and brown sugar in a microwave-safe jug and melt for 1 minute on High (100%). Stir through the ginger and flour.

3 Cut two sheets of non-stick baking paper to the size of the microwave turntable. Place 6 separate teaspoons of Brandy Snap mixture around the edge of each sheet.

4 Cook each sheet on High (100%) for 3 minutes, or until bubbling. Leave for a few seconds; remove and wrap the snaps around a rolling pin. As they cool, the snaps harden and can be removed. Serve with Rhubarb Fool.

Lightly fold the whipped cream and custard into the rhubarb purée.

Put the butter, brown sugar and golden syrup in a microwave-safe jug.

Place six teaspoons of mixture on the baking paper, leaving room to spread.

Wrap the cooked Brandy Snaps around a rolling pin while they are still soft.

MERINGUE BERRY TORTE

Preparation time: 20 minutes
Total cooking time: 5 minutes
Serves 6

4 egg whites
3/4 cup (185 g/6 oz) caster sugar
1 cup (250 ml/8 fl oz) cream, whipped
300 g (9 2/3 oz) mixed berries, sliced

1 Line a 19 x 32 cm (8 x 13 inch) microwave-safe dish with non-stick baking paper. Place the egg whites in a large dry bowl and beat until soft peaks form. Gradually add the sugar, beating well after each addition. Beat for 4 minutes, or until thick and glossy and the sugar has dissolved.
2 Spread the mixture into the prepared dish and cook on Medium (50%) for 5 minutes, or until firm to touch. Turn out onto baking paper sprinkled with a little caster sugar. Remove the top layer of baking paper.
3 Cut the meringue in two. Place one half on a serving plate, spread with half the cream and top with half the berries. Top with the remaining meringue half. Spread with the remaining cream and decorate with the remaining berries. Dust with icing sugar if you prefer sweetened berries, and cut into squares to serve.

COOK'S FILE

Hint: Always use a clean dry bowl for beating egg whites—the slightest hint of grease will stop them aerating.
Note: This Torte has a gooey marshmallow texture rather than a crisp finish.

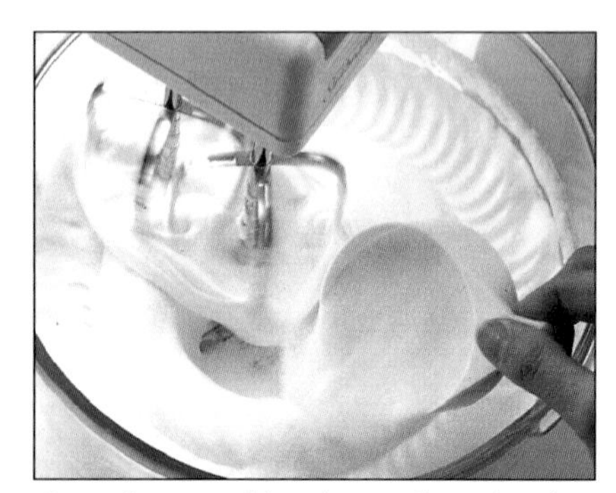

Beat the egg whites into soft peaks, then gradually beat in the sugar.

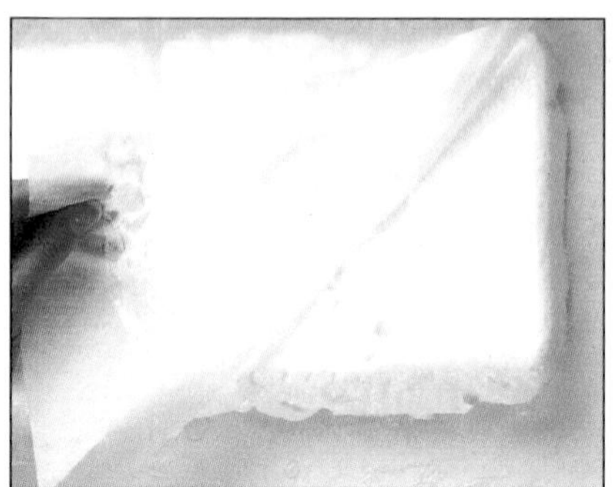

Turn out the meringue and peel away the piece of baking paper.

Cut the meringue in half and top one layer with cream and half the berries.

INDEX

INTERNATIONAL GLOSSARY

tomato paste (Aus)	tomato purée (UK)
snow pea	mange tout
capsicum	red or green pepper
bicarbonate of soda	baking soda
choc bits	chocolate chips
eggplant	aubergine
zucchini	courgette
lima beans	butter beans
tomato purée (Aus)	sieved crushed tomatoes/ passata (UK)
green prawns	raw prawns
dark chocolate	plain chocolate
thick cream	double cream
cream	single cream
silver beet	Swiss chard
apricot nectar	apricot juice

Published by Murdoch Books®, a division of Murdoch Magazines Pty Limited, 213 Miller Street, North Sydney NSW 2060.

Managing Editor: Jane Price **Designer:** Michele Lichtenberger **Food Editors:** Kerrie Ray, Tracy Rutherford, Jody Vassallo **Recipe Development:** Kerrie Mullins, Sally Parker **Home Economists:** Michelle Earl, Kerrie Mullins, Michelle Lawton **Photographers:** Tony Lyon, Reg Morrison (step photography) **Food Stylist:** Carolyn Fienberg **Food Preparation:** Jo Forrest
Publisher: Anne Wilson **International Sales Manager:** Mark Newman

National Library of Australia Cataloguing-in-Publication Data. Successful Microwave Recipes. Includes index. ISBN 0 86411 535 0. 1. Microwave Cookery (Series: Family Circle step-by-step) 641.5882 First printed 1996.
Printed by Prestige Litho, Queensland.

Distributed in the UK by Australian Consolidated Press (UK) Ltd, 20 Galowhill Road, Brackmills, Northampton NN4 0EE. Enquiries: 01604 760456. Distributed in NZ by Golden Press, a division of HarperCollins Publishers, 31 View Road, Glenfield, PO Box 1, Auckland 1.